MASTER EFFECTIVE COMMUNICATION

11 FOUNDATIONAL STRATEGIES TO STRENGTHEN YOUR INTERPERSONAL SKILLS, UNLEASH THE POWER OF STORYTELLING, AND LEARN TO TALK TO ANYONE, ANYWHERE

MARGUERITE ALLOLDING

© Copyright 2023. All rights reserved.

The content contained within this book may not be reproduced, duplicated, or transmitted without direct written permission from the author or the publisher.

Under no circumstances will any blame or legal responsibility be held against the publisher, or author, for any damages, reparation, or monetary loss due to the information contained within this book. Either directly or indirectly. You are responsible for your own choices, actions, and results.

Legal Notice:

This book is copyright protected. This book is only for personal use. You cannot amend, distribute, sell, use, quote, or paraphrase any part of this book's content without the author's or publisher's consent.

Disclaimer Notice:

Please note that the information contained within this document is for educational and entertainment purposes only. All effort has been made to present accurate, up-to-date, reliable, and complete information. No warranties of any kind are declared or implied. Readers acknowledge that the author is not engaging in rendering legal, financial, medical, or professional advice. The content within this book has been derived from various sources. Please consult a licensed professional before attempting any techniques outlined in this book.

By reading this document, the reader agrees that under no circumstances is the author responsible for any losses, direct or indirect, which are incurred because of the use of the information contained within this document, including, but not limited to, — errors, omissions, or inaccuracies.

1st Editon

Author: Marguerite Allolding

Publisher: She Leads Strategies, LLC

CONTENTS

Introduction	vii
1. BRIDGING THE GAP – UNDERSTAND THE BASICS OF COMMUNICATION	1
Types of Communication: Verbal, Non-Verbal, and Written	3
The Impact of Effective Communication on Relationships and Success	6
The Need for Adaptability in Communication	9
2. NAVIGATING THE SOCIAL SEAS: UNLEASHING YOUR SOCIAL INTELLIGENCE	11
The Role of Empathy in Social Intelligence	13
Boosting Your Social Intelligence	14
Social Intelligence in the Digital World	17
The Impact of Social Intelligence on Your Life	18
3. BREAKING DOWN WALLS: OVERCOME COMMUNICATION BARRIERS	21
Tuning into the Right Frequency: Overcoming Misunderstandings	23
Bridging the Gap: Navigating Cultural Differences in Communication	24
The Noise Within: Overcoming Internal Distractions	27
Blocking Out the Noise: Managing External Distractions	29
4. THE SILENT LANGUAGE: DECIPHER NON-VERBAL COMMUNICATION	31
Body Talk: Deciphering Body Language	32
Face Value: Interpreting Facial Expressions	35
Eye Contact: The Window to the Soul	37
The Power of Touch: Understanding Haptic Communication	39
Dress to Impress: The Role of Appearance in Non-Verbal Communication	42
The Space Between Us: Understanding Proxemics	43
The Sound of Silence: The Role of Silence in Non-Verbal Communication	45

5. SPOKEN WORD SYMPHONY - MASTER VERBAL COMMUNICATION ... 47
   Tone Tune-Up: The Influence of Tone in Communication ... 48
   Listening Ears: The Art of Active Listening ... 51
   The Power of Pause: Using Silence Effectively in Verbal Communication ... 52

6. CRAFTING WORDS THAT RESONATE: CONQUER WRITTEN COMMUNICATION ... 54
   Improving Your Writing Skills ... 55
   Adapting Your Writing for Different Contexts ... 56
   The Role of Technology in Written Communication ... 58
   Write and Wrong: Common Mistakes and How to Avoid Them ... 60

7. BOOSTING YOUR SELF-BELIEF: THE CONFIDENCE CONNECTION ... 62
   Strategies to Boost Your Confidence ... 63
   Overcoming Communication Anxiety ... 64
   Cultivating Confidence Through Personal Growth ... 65

8. COMMANDING THE ROOM: THE ROADMAP TO RIVETING PRESENTATIONS ... 67
   Facing the Fear: Tackling Stage Fright ... 70
   Powerful Visual Aids: More Than Just Pretty Pictures ... 71
   Mastering Q&A Sessions ... 72
   The Art of Storytelling in Presentations ... 73

9. UNLEASH THE POWER OF STORYTELLING IN COMMUNICATION ... 75
   Crafting Your Story: The Essential Elements ... 76
   Storytelling Techniques for Effective Communication ... 79
   The Role of Storytelling in Different Forms of Communication ... 81
   Storytelling in Practice: From Boardrooms to Coffee Breaks ... 83
   Overcoming Storytelling Hurdles: Mastering the Art ... 84

10. NAVIGATE DIGITAL COMMUNICATION: THE NEW NORMAL ... 86
    The Challenges of Digital Communication ... 88
    Strategies for Effective Digital Communication ... 88
    Tools and Platforms for Enhancing Digital Communication ... 91
    The Future of Digital Communication ... 92

11. **THE ART OF CONVERSING: LEARNING TO TALK TO ANYONE, ANYWHERE** — 93
   Breaking the Ice: Starting Conversations — 94
   Maintaining the Momentum: Sustaining Conversations — 95
   Navigating Through Awkward Silences — 96
   Mastering Small Talk: The Building Block of Conversations — 98
   Conversing Across Cultures: Embracing Diversity — 99
   Overcoming Communication Barriers: Talking to Difficult People — 100
   Adapting Communication Styles: Different Strokes for Different Folks — 101

   Conclusion — 105
   About the Author — 109
   Also by Marguerite Allolding — 111
   References — 115

INTRODUCTION

Can you relate to this scenario? The one where you're standing before what felt like the firing squad of upper management, tasked with making a presentation, even though you know the project like the back of your hand, words escape you like air from a punctured balloon, leaving behind a flustered mess of mumbles and stammers.

I can certainly relate. As someone who has faced such a feared scenario, I can tell you that it led to a lightbulb moment for me. Effective communication in the professional realm is not just a nice-to-have skill. It's an absolute must-have.

This book is the fruit of that cringe-worthy realization. It's crafted for anyone who's ever found themselves wishing for a rewind button after a conversation, presentation, or even a simple email. The goal is to transform you into a communication maestro adept at navigating the sophisticated dance of professional discourse, whether in the boardroom, at a social event, or anywhere in between.

What sets this guide apart is its unwavering commitment to practicality, accessibility, and a touch of humor. I'm not here to bore you with jargon or abstract theories. Instead, I'm diving headfirst into the nitty-gritty of real-life examples, case studies, and interactive exercises designed to sharpen your communication skills until they're as smooth as a well-oiled machine.

Structured in four comprehensive parts, this book lays the foundation with the basics of effective communication and then builds on that with insights into verbal, non-verbal, and written exchanges. From there, we escalate to advanced strategies for ensuring your message doesn't just leave your mouth but lands with impact. And because we live in a world brimming with unique communication challenges, there's a whole section dedicated to these particular topics—think digital communication etiquette, cross-cultural conversations, and even how to navigate the treacherous waters of conflict resolution.

If you're thinking, "Great, another book that promises to change my life," I understand your reluctance to get roped into empty promises. I was you once as I searched for answers. But please, hear me out. I created what I could not find because I needed it and felt that others were like me. We sometimes have to be straight-faced and oh-so-serious at work. This book is your place to be comfortable as you learn. With a sprinkle of humor to keep things light and a ton of actionable advice, this isn't just another self-help manual destined to pick up dust on your bookshelf. It was created to be your new best friend in the quest for communication prowess at work.

It doesn't stop at the office door, though. The insights and techniques you'll discover here can transform how you connect with everyone in your life. From deepening relationships with family and friends to navigating social situations with ease, this book is designed to enhance your interpersonal skills across the board. Imagine approaching every conversation with confidence, whether it's a tough negotiation at work or a heartfelt chat over coffee. You are not limited to only professional growth. Acting on this advice will enrich every interaction you have, making life richer, more fulfilling, and, yes, even more fun.

Being an effective communicator is an ever-evolving process based on the simple virtue that our world is constantly changing. So, while the basics might remain universal, see this as a road that never truly ends. As we embark on this journey together, I invite you to lean into the discomfort of uncharted territory. This path to mastering effective communication is much like learning to dance—awkward at first but oh-so graceful once you find your rhythm. Even when times change, having the fundamentals to guide you will allow you to flow with the rhythm. And who knows? By the end of this book, you might just be ready to take that metaphorical stage and leave your audience, whether it's one or one hundred, utterly spellbound.

With that, I urge you to flip the page and step into the world of effective communication. Together, we'll explore the art and science of making your words count, ensuring that never again will you find yourself wishing for a rewind button. Let's turn that presentation of dread into a triumph of eloquence and impact. Ready? Let's dive in.

1

BRIDGING THE GAP – UNDERSTAND THE BASICS OF COMMUNICATION

Some people just seem to have a magic touch when it comes to getting their point across or making everyone feel at ease in a conversation, don't they? This natural ability to connect effortlessly with others is a fascinating blend of psychological, neurological, and social factors. This knack for connection is not just a singular skill but a complex interplay of various components of human behavior and cognition.

Even if you're not one of the people who are gifted naturally with this aptitude, it is something you can learn. All skills are learned behaviors that anyone who is determined and studious can study and put into practice.

Effective communication is more than having a way with words or being a chatterbox. The true essence of effective communication is understanding the full spectrum of how we exchange information and energy with each other.

The problem many of us face in becoming effective communicators is that we focus so heavily on what is said that we miss out on the remaining parts that contribute to the interaction. How someone throws their voice, the speed at which they're talking, and even pauses can spill the beans on what they're trying to say. Those make up the verbal part of communication. There is also what is not being enunciated. The way they stand, move their hands or make expressions send a bunch of stealthy signals our way. These silent hints tell us what's going on in their head, backing up or bashing what they're saying.

There's a study done by a psychologist named Albert Mehrabian back in the '70s at UCLA. It backs up the fact that communication is not just what you say but how you say it. He discovered that when we're chatting face-to-face, the words we use are just the tip of the iceberg. What truly tells the tale is our body language and how we say those words. He called his findings the 7-38-55 rule of communication.

To break it down, Mehrabian figured that the actual words only make up about 7% of what we're getting across in personal conversations. The way we say those words—like our tone—counts for 38%, and our body language takes the lion's share at 55%.

Especially when someone's words don't quite match up with how they're acting, we're way more likely to believe the silent message they're sending. For instance, if you sound super excited and your eyes light up at the prospect of hanging out with your friend, this person will feel that this meetup will be a highlight of your day. But if you mumble it while scrolling through your phone, they might think that you're not that into it.

This concept isn't just for personal relations. It plays out big time in the professional world, too. Consider Steve Jobs, the Apple wizard. His presentations weren't just successful because of the innovative products (though, that helped). Jobs was a master of using his voice, his gestures, and his timing to truly connect with his audience and inspire his team. He wasn't just sharing information. He was telling a story, creating an experience that resonated on an emotional level. That's the power of understanding and leveraging all aspects of communication.

You can leverage this power, too, by getting the basics of communication down. That goes beyond learning to talk well. It's about understanding that communication is a multi-layered process involving our words, how we say them, and our non-verbal cues. A good combination of these elements will not only help you convey information but also build relationships, influence decisions, and drive change. They will help you nail a job interview and lead a team to success. The benefits will spill into your daily life because effective communication makes everyday interactions more meaningful. Let's get the ball rolling on developing your skill as an effective communicator with the types of communication at your disposal and that you would learn to tune into.

Types of Communication: Verbal, Non-Verbal, and Written

Communication can be broken down into three main types. I introduced you to two of these moments ago: verbal and non-verbal. The third is written. Let's take a closer look at each type now. I will also provide a few tips for improving your communication in each section. These are all inspired by Steve Jobs!

Verbal Communication

This one is all about what we say and how we say it. Imagine you're telling a story at a party. The words you choose, the punchlines, the dramatic pauses—all that jazz is verbal communication. The story will be brought to life not by the words you use but by how you use them.

Pro tips inspired by Steve Jobs:

- **Simplicity is Key:** Jobs was all about making complex ideas easy to digest. When you're talking, choose clear, straightforward language. No need to decorate your speech with fancy jargon to sound smart.
- **Tell a Story:** Jobs knew the power of a good story. It's engaging and memorable. Whether you're presenting or just

having a conversation, frame your message as a story. It's more likely to resonate.
- **Practice Makes Perfect:** Jobs would practice relentlessly before any major presentation. Rehearse your talking points to reduce stumbles and increase confidence.
- **Engage Your Audience:** Make eye contact. Read the room. Jobs was a master at engaging with his audience, making them feel like part of the journey.
- **Passion is Persuasive:** Let your enthusiasm shine through. Jobs' passion was infectious. When you talk about something you truly care about, it shows and can sway your audience.

Non-Verbal Communication

There's a famous saying: "It's not what you say, but how you say it." That's non-verbal communication in a nutshell. It's all the signals we send without opening our mouths—like when you meet someone, and their handshake is like holding a limp fish. You instantly make assumptions about what this might mean, right? Or when someone's smiling but their eyes say, "I'd rather be anywhere but here." These non-verbal cues are the background music to our words, setting the tone and mood.

Pro tips inspired by Steve Jobs:

- **Master Your Body Language:** Adopt a posture that conveys confidence. Jobs used open body language to appear more approachable and authoritative.
- **Facial Expressions Matter:** Your face says it all. Jobs' expressions matched the tone of his message, adding an extra layer of sincerity. Smile when it's positive and show concern when it's serious.
- **Dress the Part:** Jobs had a signature look that became iconic. Your attire sends a message, too. Dress appropriately for the context to align with your verbal message.

- **Use Gestures Effectively:** Jobs used hand gestures to emphasize points. Incorporate gestures to add emphasis, but don't overdo it. Natural movements complement your words.
- **Control Your Tone:** The way Jobs modulated his voice, stressing certain words and varying his pace, kept his audience hooked. Pay attention to your tone to make your message more compelling.

Written Communication

These encompass texts, emails, tweets, and the occasional handwritten note. Written communication is a whole different ball game because you have to get your point without the help of your charming voice or expressive eyebrows. You have to choose the right words and nail the tone. Want to sound professional? You might need to ditch the emojis. Trying to be funny? Timing and context are key, and please, for everyone's sake, make sure your jokes land the way they're meant to. Tools like Grammarly or Hemingway Editor help you polish your words until they shine.

Pro tips inspired by Steve Jobs:

1. **Be Clear and Concise:** Just like his product designs, Jobs' communications were straightforward. Get to the point quickly and avoid unnecessary fluff.
2. **Focus on the Benefit:** Jobs always highlighted the benefits of Apple products. When writing, make sure your audience understands the "why" behind your message.
3. **Create Engaging Subject Lines or Titles:** Jobs was a master at grabbing attention. Use engaging headings to ensure your written communication gets noticed.
4. **Edit Ruthlessly:** Jobs was known for his perfectionism. Proofread your writing for clarity, grammar, and typos. A clean, error-free message reflects professionalism.
5. **Use Visuals:** Whenever possible, incorporate visuals. Jobs used imagery to enhance his messages. Charts, graphs, or

images can make your written communication more engaging.

Here's a fun fact: According to the folks at Pew Research Center, more than 90% of U.S. adults are firing off emails for work (Statista, 2023). It's the digital age, and written words are the unsung heroes keeping our professional world spinning.

So, whether you're chatting up a storm, mastering the art of the meaningful glance, or typing away at lightning speed, each type of communication has its rules. Knowing how to mix and match them can turn you into a communication ninja, ready to connect, impress, and express in any situation. We'll delve deeper into how to stealthily use each of these types of communication in the coming chapters.

The Impact of Effective Communication on Relationships and Success

Being an effective communicator has become quite the buzz phrase, and as with anything that goes viral these days, it's hard to get to the heart of the matter without getting sucked into the hype. So, let's step back for a moment and get a big picture of what being an effective communicator means for your life.

Imagine effective communication as a tool – the ultimate Swiss Army knife in your relationship and career toolkit. It's that all-in-one instrument that can open cans (solve problems), cut through stuff (clear misunderstandings), and even pull out corks (unlock deeper connections). Here's why it's your go-to gadget for building bridges and climbing ladders, both in life and at work.

When it comes to your closest friends or your significant other, ever noticed how a simple misunderstanding can turn into a week-long cold war? Or how a perfectly timed "I get where you're coming from" can make this take a completely different road? That's effective communication in a nutshell. It allows for "getting" each other, really getting each other. It's your decoder for your partner's or friend's thoughts and feelings.

Gary Chapman hit the nail on the head with his concept called The Five Love Languages. Each person has a unique emotional language they speak and understand best. This emotional language determines how they communicate love and prefer to receive it. Chapman identified five primary love languages:

1. **Words of Affirmation:** For some people, hearing "I love you," compliments, or verbal support feels like a warm hug for their soul. The words affirm their worth and your affection for them.
2. **Acts of Service:** For these folks, doing something helpful or taking a task off their hands says "I care" louder than any words could. They understand that easing their load in life is love.
3. **Receiving Gifts:** A thoughtful gift is a physical symbol of love and thoughtfulness in this case. The idea that someone took the time to give this person something representing their feelings touches them deeply.
4. **Quality Time:** This means giving someone your undivided attention and being truly present with them. Spending time together, with full focus on each other, creates feelings of being valued and loved.
5. **Physical Touch:** For some, physical closeness—hugs, kisses, holding hands—is the most powerful communicator of love. Connection and reassurance are communicated through touch.

If you know your partner's love language, you can express your love in a way they understand and appreciate deeply. For instance, if their primary love language is Acts of Service, doing something as simple as taking over dinner preparation or fixing something for them can make them feel incredibly loved and valued. On the flip side, no matter how many gifts you give to someone whose love language is Words of Affirmation, they might not feel as loved until they hear you say how much you appreciate and love them.

The concept of love languages, while initially designed to enhance romantic relationships, is incredibly effective in all types of relationships—be it with family members, friends, or even colleagues. Understanding and applying the five love languages beyond the romantic sphere can significantly improve communication, deepen connections, and foster a greater sense of appreciation and understanding among individuals.

So, while the context might differ, giving thoughtful gifts can also apply in professional settings. A small, thoughtful gift for a colleague who's going through a tough time or celebrating a personal milestone can communicate respect and camaraderie.

Speaking of the professional world, ever wondered why some companies, like the Googles and Amazons of the world, seem to keep winning? Sure, they've got smart people and cool products, but top-notch communication is at the heart of it all. These companies are like well-oiled machines, where every part knows what the other is doing and why. They hire folks who can talk the talk and walk the walk because they know that's how you get teams to click, ideas to spark, and projects to cross the finish line.

Amazon's Leadership Principles explicitly list "Earns Trust of Others" and "Are Right, A Lot". These ideologies underscore the value of clear, honest, and effective communication. As such, Amazon isn't just about delivering your packages on time. They deliver on effective communication, ensuring their teams are on the same page, trust each other, and make decisions that hit the mark more often than not.

Gallup found that companies that communicate like champs aren't just making their employees happier. They're making more money. I'm talking about 47% higher returns to shareholders. That's not chump change. With everyone in the loop and rowing in the same direction, these companies navigate through rough waters much more efficiently.

So, whether you're trying to make peace with your partner over who forgot to take out the trash, or you're presenting a game-changing idea to your boss, remember: effective communication is your best bet. It builds bridges in relationships and paves roads to success. In the grand scheme of things, it's the glue that holds everything together.

The Need for Adaptability in Communication

Think of how it goes when you're chatting with your best friend, sharing jokes and stories. The energy is typically casual and easy-going for most of us. Now, picture yourself in a meeting at work, presenting a project, or discussing a task. The difference in how you communicate in these two scenarios is huge, right? That's because, instinctively, you adapt your communication style based on who you're talking to and your situation. It's like switching between different languages, except the languages are different communication styles.

The TV show 'The Office' is a goldmine of awkward, hilarious moments that perfectly illustrate what happens when people don't adjust their communication for the situation or the people they're talking to. From Michael Scott's cringe-worthy attempts at being relatable to Dwight's blunt, no-filter comments, the show is a masterclass in communication mishaps, highlighting the need for adaptability in a funny and painfully relatable way.

This adaptability comes beyond the tone or the choice of words. We also need to learn to be sensitive to cultural nuances. Imagine you're in a business meeting with international colleagues. In some cultures, making direct eye contact is a sign of confidence and respect; in others, it might be seen as aggressive or rude. Recognizing and adapting to these cultural differences comes from understanding that what works in one context might not fly in another.

Forbes emphasizes adaptability as the most important communication skill in the workplace. And they're not wrong. Whether navigating cultural sensitivities, switching gears between professional and personal settings, or just figuring out the best way to convey your message to different audiences, adapting your communication style is key. It's what helps avoid those "that did not go as planned" moments and ensures your message isn't just heard but understood, no matter who you're talking to or where you are.

2

NAVIGATING THE SOCIAL SEAS: UNLEASHING YOUR SOCIAL INTELLIGENCE

Mentally place yourself at a huge party. The atmosphere is full of chatter and laughter. Everyone is having a good time. See yourself moving around from group to group, talking and interacting like a bee moving from flower to flower. You're mingling, but this movement is not just motivated by the aim of socializing. What you're really doing is practicing social intelligence.

It's all good and well to be the life of the party (if your social battery has that capacity) and to have a great chat with someone. It is even better when you learn the skill of reading the room. Then, you can understand what makes each person tick and respond in ways that create a positive vibe for everyone involved.

Social intelligence is like being a social detective. You're not just hearing words. You're tuning into emotions, body language, and the unsaid things between the lines. Daniel Goleman, a psychologist, author, and all-around expert on emotional intelligence, says that social intelligence has two major parts: social awareness and social facility. Social awareness is your ability to get what others are feeling and thinking. It's like having an emotional radar that picks up on the subtleties. Social facility, on the other hand, is the application of this skill to interact smoothly with others.

Let's put it in a work context. You're a leader in your team, and you want your team to be engaged and productive. Goleman, in a Harvard Business Review article, talked about how leaders with high social intelligence create what he calls "resonant" relationships. Being highly socially intelligent puts you in harmony with your team, meaning there's mutual understanding and respect. The feel-good stuff is a bonus, but the real prizes are measurable results like better engagement and higher productivity.

Further research backs this up, showing that social intelligence is crucial for effective leadership communication. Great leadership is not just about giving orders or making decisions. You have to learn to connect with your team, understand their perspectives, and communicate in a way that resonates with them.

Social intelligence supersedes the realm of our jobs and careers. In everyday life, harnessing the power of social intelligence means you become that person who not only talks but listens - really listens. You catch onto the subtle cues in a conversation, adapt your approach based on the vibe of the group or person you are relating to, and respond in a way that builds trust and connection. Whether in a boardroom or at a backyard barbecue, social intelligence helps you create meaningful connections and make every interaction count.

Think of social intelligence aptitude as learning to ride a bike. At first, it might seem tricky. You're wobbling and feel like you're about to fall off at any moment. But just like bike riding, social intelligence is a skill you can improve with practice. Sure, there are 'naturals' – the people who seem to effortlessly charm everyone. But social intelligence is not hoarded by them alone. It's for anyone willing to put in the effort. It starts with little steps, like paying more attention to how people react during conversations, listening more than you talk, and noticing the mood in a room. These actions are the reps that build your social muscle. Just like working out your physical muscles, the more you use it, the stronger it gets. This chapter familiarizes you with the reps you need to build your social muscles.

The Role of Empathy in Social Intelligence

Not many people enter adulthood without walking around in their parents' shoes as kids. I remember doing so in my mother's heels. As I clicked and clacked along the floor of our home, I thought I could see the world from her viewpoint. I would imagine being a mommy and a career woman. I saw myself baking cookies that my future kids loved just like she did and even scolded these future offspring (my dolls all lined up in a row) for being naughty like I was at times. My imaginings were so strong I thought I was really feeling what she was feeling.

I did not know it back then but what I was feeling was empathy. It is the ability that supports social intelligence. It's what allows you to step into their shoes so you understand them better and share their emotions, almost as if they were your own. Practice empathy lets you hear more than just what another person says and tunes you into the feelings behind them. You almost instinctively get what others need and why they feel the way they do. This doesn't just make conversations better. It makes them more meaningful.

Showing empathy as a manager or in any other leadership position allows you to lead from a position where you genuinely understand and care about your team. This will not go unnoticed. A study by the Center for Creative Leadership found that empathetic managers are often seen as better performers by their bosses. Empathy is a pop of color in a sea of black and white that makes leaders stand out.

Even big names in the business world swear by the power of empathy. Take, for example, Satya Nadella, the CEO of Microsoft. He's a tech giant, but when he talks about what's driving Microsoft's success, it's not just about software or innovation. In his book "Hit Refresh," he credits empathy as a key factor. He believes that understanding and connecting with the feelings of others is necessary, not just in leadership, but in shaping how a company moves forward.

Empathy is the bridge that connects you with others. As a singular skill, this means not trying to fix their problems or giving advice. The defining quality of being empathetic is being there, really being there, in that moment with them. You're listening, understanding, and feeling with them. Whether you're a manager, a friend, or just someone who wants to connect better with people, empathy is your tool for building deeper, more authentic relationships. With empathy, you make everyone you interact with feel seen, heard, and understood.

Boosting Your Social Intelligence

We tend to get on the younger generation's back about being glued to video games, but we can learn a thing or two from them. In many ways, if we treated life like a game, we could level up quicker than looking at it as a tedious chore that we have to get through. So, let's treat boosting your social intelligence as leveling up in a video game in this game of life. To climb the rank, you need to sharpen the abilities that let you connect, understand, and vibe with people on a deeper level. Sharpening your social intelligence blade involves using tools like:

- Observation
- Active Listening
- Empathy

Let's look at how you can obtain each of these tools individually.

Observation

First off, observation. This social antenna lets you pick up the signals that other people are casting off through body language and tone of voice. Activating your observation prowess means you notice when your friend says they're fine, but their crossed arms and forced smile scream the opposite. At a family dinner, this could look like noticing a sibling is unusually quiet and picks at their food. This might indicate they're upset or something is on their mind. This is useful in all social situations you might find yourself in. Let's say you're at the office and during a team meeting, one colleague constantly checks the clock and another seems ready to interject but hesitates. These cues might suggest time sensitivity for one and perhaps a lack of confidence or uncertainty in the other. Or let's say you're at a networking event and notice someone standing alone, looking around nervously. This could mean they're feeling out of place or shy – an opportunity for you to perhaps help this person fit in.

Want a fun way to practice your observation skills even before you have to in real-life situations? Cue up episodes of "Friends" or "The Big Bang Theory." As you watch, try to guess how a character is feeling or what they might do next based on their non-verbal cues. It's like a game of emotional detective, and these shows are your training ground.

Active Listening

Next on the list of tools you need to gather to level up your social intelligence game is active listening. Listening to another person is more than just hearing what they say. To fully connect with the verbal conversation, you need to be fully present and communicate that through your words and actions. Show you're engaged – nod, make eye contact, occasionally repeat what this person has said – and absorb what they're saying. To brush up on this skill, podcasts like "The Art of Charm" are gold. They're packed with actionable tips you can try out in your next convo, turning you into the friend everyone feels really heard by.

More ways that you can practice active listening include asking open-ended questions. Let's set up a scenario to show what they could look like. You're on a coffee date with a friend who insists everything's great. Yet, you notice they're avoiding eye contact and fidgeting with their cup. Asking an open-ended question to probe into what they're feeling might sound like, "How have you really been feeling?" Hopefully, this encourages them to open up. If that is the case, show genuine interest in their response. Reflect what you've heard to show you're engaged, "It sounds like you've had a lot on your plate."

Asking for opinions is another way of showing that you're actively listening. At the office, this is especially important to practice with team members who seem hesitant. When they do make contributions, actively acknowledge them with phrases like, "That's an interesting point. Can you expand on that?"

Being an active listener also means making a safe space in your company. This can look like expressing concern and projecting an open, friendly demeanor. For example, let's go back to the situation where the person was standing alone at the networking event. You could approach them with a friendly greeting and ask about their interest in the event. Focus on their responses and ask follow-up questions to keep the conversation flowing.

Build on your display of active listening by showing empathy. Share your own experiences of feeling nervous at such events to make them feel less alone. We emphasized the importance of empathy in social intelligence earlier. Now, it's time to put it into practice. There is one powerful activity that I think makes anyone more empathetic: volunteering. For instance, getting out there and helping at a local community center exposes you to a wide array of life experiences and perspectives. It's a reality check that opens your heart and mind, helping you connect with people on a level that goes way beyond words.

With these tools in hand, you are fully equipped to boost your social intelligence in this game called life. To clarify, boosting your social intelligence isn't about becoming someone you're not. That is a common misconception we must debunk earlier so that the mistake does not hinder your efforts down the line. Rather, deliberate action is about enhancing the best parts of you by becoming more observant, a better listener, and deeply empathetic. The real-world practices brought up in this section are not just meant to make you a better communicator. They will help you become a better human.

Social Intelligence in the Digital World

In the day and age that we live in, social interactions are not limited to face-to-face interactions anymore. Technology has expanded that to mean so many more things – emails, text messages, DMs, social media comments, and more. This means that leveling up our social intelligence game also includes cracking the code of digital chitchat.

Think about it...how many times have you misinterpreted a text because it was missing that crucial eye roll emoji? Or read an email in the wrong tone and have a mini heart attack?

You're not just missing the ball with these examples of miscommunication in these digital formats. These modes of communication have different characteristics compared to person-to-person exchanges. First off, understanding the "tone" in digital communication is like trying to read a book without seeing the characters' expressions. You're relying solely on words, which can sometimes be as clear as mud. Ever sent an email that was meant to be funny but ended up causing a World War III-level misunderstanding?

Luckily, you don't have to wade in this pool of obscurity indefinitely. Tools like Tone Analyzer by IBM Watson make these forms of communication clearer. It sniffs out the tone of your messages before you hit send, saving you from many "Oops, I didn't mean it that way" moments.

Being aware of and utilizing digital etiquette and the unwritten rules of online communication will also save you from digital faux pas. Typing in ALL CAPS might feel like you're emphasizing your point, but you're virtually yelling at the person on the other end. Nobody likes being yelled at. The online equivalent of holding the door open for someone includes simple gestures, like using please and thank you in emails or acknowledging messages with a quick emoji. They might be simple, but they can make digital communication feel more human.

Reading is a human activity that just might help you increase your online social intelligence. Psychology Today suggests that curling up with good literary fiction sharpens your ability to empathize and understand others. When you're engrossed in the lives of Elizabeth Bennet or Holden Caulfield, you're not just escaping reality. You're training your brain to navigate complex social relationships, even digital ones. You're working out for your empathy muscles, preparing you to read between the lines of tweets, texts, and posts.

In this digital world, being socially intelligent means more than just knowing when to post a witty comment. You're fine-tuning your ability to communicate clearly, understand the emotional undertones of digital chatter, and maintain the niceties that make interactions pleasant, whether face-to-face or screen-to-screen.

The Impact of Social Intelligence on Your Life

Being socially intelligent adds a dash of charm to your ability to have small talk effectively, sure. However, the benefits extend further. When you deeply understand and connect with those around you, both at home and at work, good relations are turned into great ones.

In your personal life, let's say you're trying to figure out the perfect gift for your partner. Instead of defaulting to the usual suspects (flowers, chocolates, the latest tech gadget), you remember that chapter from "The Five Love Languages" you read. You realize your partner thrives on quality time. So, you plan a day out together doing their favorite activities. It's not about the monetary value but the thought and understanding behind it.

Beyond the romance department, social intelligence comes in handy. Here are a few scenarios depicting these.

Scenario 1: Celebrating a Friend's Achievement

Your friend just landed their dream job, and you're thinking of how to celebrate. Instead of just sending a congratulatory text or buying a generic gift, you remember they mentioned how nervous they were about making a good impression. Using your social intelligence, you decide to put together a "First Day Survival Kit" filled with their favorite snacks, a motivational notebook, and a good luck charm. It's a thoughtful way to show you listened and understand their excitement and nerves.

Scenario 2: A Family Get-Together

It's the holiday season, and you're hosting a family get-together. You know that certain topics can lead to heated debates between family members. With your social intelligence, you steer conversations toward common interests and shared happy memories, creating a positive atmosphere. When the conversation starts drifting toward potential conflict zones, you tactfully introduce a fun, engaging activity everyone enjoys, like a board game or a trip down memory lane with old photo albums. This approach keeps the mood light and the day enjoyable for everyone.

Scenario 3: Helping a Neighbor

You notice your usually cheerful neighbor seems down. Instead of prying or making assumptions, you offer a listening ear over a cup of coffee. They open up about feeling lonely since their children moved out. Remembering they have a passion for gardening, you suggest joining a local gardening club together. This act of empathy and understanding not only lifts their spirits but also helps them find a community with similar interests, enriching their social life.

I create these scenarios to show you a real-world view of what social intelligence looks like – you can forge deeper connections with those around you by truly understanding what makes them tick.

Now, let's switch scenes to your professional life. Imagine your workplace is a team sport, where being a star player isn't just about how good you are with numbers or how innovative your ideas are. It's about how well you play with others. A report by the Institute for Corporate Productivity isn't just throwing numbers around when it says collaborative companies outperform others. It highlights a truth we've all felt: teams that communicate effectively, understand each other's strengths and weaknesses, and work together seamlessly do better. And at the heart of this is social intelligence. It helps you read the room during a meeting, offer support to a stressed colleague without them having to ask, or lead your team to success because you know how to motivate and inspire them.

The Wall Street Journal called social intelligence "The Secret to Career Success." Top performers aren't just skilled at their jobs. They know how to navigate the complex web of relationships in the workplace. They understand their colleagues, can mediate conflicts, and inspire loyalty and respect. Don't mistake this for being manipulative or fake. True social intelligence means genuinely connecting with people, understanding their perspectives, and working together towards common goals.

So, whether you're trying to make your partner's day a little brighter or aiming to climb the career ladder, boosting your social intelligence lets you see beyond the surface, understand the emotional undercurrents of your interactions, and respond in ways that build stronger, more meaningful connections. In a world that's increasingly digital and sometimes impersonal, these skills are more valuable than ever. But what happens when despite our best efforts, we find ourselves facing walls instead of windows in our conversations? The next chapter dives into how to tear down communication barriers.

3

BREAKING DOWN WALLS: OVERCOME COMMUNICATION BARRIERS

We've all been in that place where we felt like we had something important to say but just couldn't muster up the courage to speak out. It could have been because we were worried about stumbling over our words. Perhaps the fear of being judged by our peers kept our thoughts locked up tight. Whatever the reason it happened to you, the important thing to remember is that you're not alone. 85% of people admit to clamping up in professional settings, according to a LinkedIn survey (Vilkė, V. 2023).

This silence isn't just a simple matter of awkwardness. It's a roadblock on the path to innovation and engagement in the workplace. Many brilliant ideas and solutions never see the light of day because they're trapped in the minds of those too scared to share them. Harvard Business Review even pointed out how this fear can throttle a company's growth, turning vibrant brainstorming sessions into silent, missed opportunities.

So, how do we break through this wall of silence and fear? There's no flipping a magical switch and suddenly becoming a fearless orator, I'm afraid. What you can do is take small, practical steps toward building the confidence to express yourself.

You wouldn't run a marathon without a bit of training, right? The same goes for speaking up. Begin by sharing your thoughts in settings that feel more comfortable and less intimidating, like a casual book club or a community meeting. These low-stakes environments are the perfect training ground for your voice.

You have to confront the jitters at some point, too. Techniques like deep breathing, mindfulness, and visualization can help calm your nerves. Picture yourself successfully sharing your ideas, and focus on the calm and relief that follows. You must convince your brain that speaking up isn't a saber-toothed tiger to be fought or fled from.

That will not happen if you're a mess of nerves. You can do this simple yet effective deep breathing exercise right at your desk or before a big meeting to calm those butterflies:

- Find a quiet spot or even just a moment at your desk where you won't be disturbed. Ensure your feet are flat on the ground.
- Place one hand on your abdomen, right above your belly button. This will help you focus on deep abdominal breathing rather than shallow chest breathing.
- Slowly inhale through your nose, counting to four. Feel your belly rise under your hand, filling your lungs with air. Imagine drawing calmness into your body.
- Hold your breath for a count of four. Don't clamp down or tense up. Maintain a gentle pause before you exhale.
- Exhale through your mouth for a count of four, letting your belly fall. Picture the stress and butterflies flying out with your breath.
- Repeat this cycle four times. Inhale through the nose, hold, and exhale through the mouth, all to the count of four.
- After your final exhale, take a moment to sit quietly. Notice how your body feels more relaxed and your mind clearer.

This exercise is a quick reset button, helping you clear your mind, ease anxiety, and approach your tasks or meetings with a calmer, more focused mindset. All it takes is a minute or two. The more you practice, the more second nature it will become, making it easier to harness calmness whenever those workplace jitters arise.

And don't underestimate the power of a mentor or a coach. These communication Yodas can offer you personalized feedback, helping you hone your message and delivery. They've been in the trenches and can guide you through the minefield of public speaking and assertive communication. Even if you have not already found a communication coach to help you, this chapter contains several strategies to help you break through the wall of miscommunication.

Tuning into the Right Frequency: Overcoming Misunderstandings

Don't you just hate it when the radio tunes into two different stations at the same time? The resulting noise makes it hard to understand anything. That's what misunderstandings in communication can feel like—being on competing wavelengths. There is more to it than what you're saying. You have to make sure the tunes don't get mixed up along the way. After all, a simple moment of miscommunication can lead to the kind of unnecessary drama and confusion that nobody wants, especially at work.

A study by CPP Inc., the brilliant minds behind the Myers-Briggs personality test, pinpointed misunderstandings as prime culprits behind workplace conflicts. Just a little static in the signal, and suddenly, the office is a battleground over something that could have been crystal clear from the start.

To fine-tune your communication to avoid these mix-ups, the first order of business is keeping your message clear and simple. You're not trying to win a poetry contest. You're trying to get a point across. Speak plainly, and you'll find that your message not only lands but sticks. That means – in the right context, like meetings with people outside your industry, you might have to avoid jargon or industry-specific terminologies.

Also, it helps to reiterate the key points of what you've said. A great show of this in action is wrapping up meetings with a summary to ensure everyone's caught onto the gist of your message. Don't just broadcast this message, either. Invite your audience to engage with you. Encourage questions and feedback to ensure that what you're putting out there gets picked up correctly. Asking something as simple as "Does that make sense?" can open up the floor for clarifications and ensure everyone's tuning into the same station. At the end of the day, we all want to be part of a workplace that hits the right notes together, creating harmony instead of noise.

Bridging the Gap: Navigating Cultural Differences in Communication

In the vast, interconnected world of today, understanding cultural nuances is essential, especially in professional settings. These differences can lead to misunderstandings and even conflicts in the global business arena, often stemming from varying communication styles, norms, values, and interpretations. Here's a breakdown of how these differences can cause friction:

Communication Styles

- **Direct vs. Indirect:** In some cultures, people communicate directly and value straightforwardness. In contrast, others may use more indirect communication, where the true meaning needs to be inferred. For example, direct criticism in one culture might be considered rude or insensitive in another, leading to hurt feelings or offense.
- **High-Context vs. Low-Context:** High-context cultures rely heavily on non-verbal cues and the context of the conversation to convey meaning, while low-context cultures depend on explicit verbal communication. Misinterpretations can arise when a message intended to be understood through context is taken at face value by someone from a low-context culture.

Norms and Etiquette

- **Meeting Etiquette:** The way meetings are conducted can vary greatly. For instance, the expectation of punctuality, the importance of hierarchical structures during discussions, and the approach to decision-making can differ. A perceived lack of respect for these norms might offend parties from certain cultures.
- **Negotiation Tactics:** Cultures differ in their approach to negotiations. Some may value aggressive bargaining and see it as a sign of strength, while others may find such tactics disrespectful or confrontational, favoring consensus-building instead.

Values and Attitudes

- **Power Distance:** Cultures with high power distance see hierarchical structures as natural and expect a clear distinction between different levels of authority. In contrast, cultures with low power distance value equality and are more comfortable questioning authority. Misunderstandings can arise when these inherent beliefs clash, such as when a junior employee from a low power distance culture directly challenges a senior executive from a high power distance culture.
- **Individualism vs. Collectivism:** Individualistic cultures prioritize personal goals and autonomy, whereas collectivistic cultures emphasize group harmony and collective goals. This fundamental difference can lead to conflicts in team dynamics and decision-making processes.

Interpretations and Assumptions

- **Non-Verbal Cues:** Gestures, eye contact, and physical proximity carry different meanings across cultures. For instance, a businessperson expecting a clear verbal

agreement might misinterpret a non-verbal cue of agreement as indecision or even disagreement, leading to confusion in negotiations.
- **Assumptions and Stereotypes:** Misunderstandings can also stem from preconceived notions or stereotypes about a particular culture. These assumptions may lead to misinterpretation of actions and intentions, causing conflict.

These are only a few of the possible points of conflict across cultures. To mitigate these issues, businesses need to foster cultural awareness and sensitivity among their employees. This can involve training programs focused on cross-cultural communication, encouraging open dialogue about cultural differences, and implementing strategies tailored to navigating these complexities.

The responsibility is also on us individuals to bridge the cultural gap. It starts with a bit of homework. Learn about other cultures, their norms, and how they communicate. Books like "Cultures and Organizations: Software of the Mind" by Geert Hofstede offer insights into the diverse ways cultures operate.

Keep an eye on the non-verbal cues. A thumbs-up can mean "all good" in some places but is a major insult in others. While non-verbal signals vary wildly across the globe, learning to read the room is universal. A raised eyebrow or a smile can tell you if you're making a faux pas or encourage you to continue.

When all else fails, just ask. If you're unsure whether your message is coming across as intended or if you're reading the signals right, it's okay to seek clarification. It shows you care enough to get it right.

Navigating cultural differences requires patience, practice, and a lot of open-mindedness. But the reward—a workplace that thrives on diversity and mutual understanding—is worth the effort.

The Noise Within: Overcoming Internal Distractions

It's not always external factors that cause miscommunication between us and others. Sometimes, it's because of what is going on within us. Ever had one of those days where your brain feels like a browser with too many tabs open? You're trying to listen to a colleague, but your mind is replaying that awkward conversation from yesterday, fretting over an upcoming deadline, and wondering what's for lunch. These are examples of internal distractions, the sneaky background noise that can derail our focus and muddy our communication faster than spilled coffee on a white shirt.

So, how do we clear the mental clutter? Practicing mindfulness is a good first step. You deliberately turn into your thoughts and tune down the noise. Meditation apps can be great for this, teaching you to observe your thoughts without getting swept away by them.

Becoming more emotionally intelligent also helps. Emotional intelligence is the ability to understand and manage your own emotions, as well as recognize and influence the emotions of others, enhancing communication and interpersonal relationships. Being emotionally intelligent allows you to stop your emotions from hijacking your ability to listen and respond thoughtfully.

Here are a few simple but effective ways to increase your emotional intelligence:

- **Practice Self-awareness**: Regularly check in with yourself to understand your emotions and how they influence your thoughts and actions.
- **Develop Empathy**: Try to see situations from others' perspectives to better understand their feelings and reactions.
- **Handle Criticism Positively**: View feedback as an opportunity for growth rather than a personal attack.
- **Manage Stress Effectively**: Learn and apply stress management techniques to maintain emotional balance.

- **Reflect on Emotional Responses:** After significant interactions or emotional events, reflect on your responses and consider what you could improve.
- **Seek Feedback:** Ask for feedback on your interactions from trusted friends, family, or colleagues to gain insights into your emotional intelligence.

Lastly, let's talk about challenging biases. We've all got them, hidden filters that color our perception of ourselves, other people, and the world at large. Biases can subtly influence decisions and interactions, often without us even realizing it. Here are some common examples:

- **Confirmation Bias:** Favoring information that confirms one's preexisting beliefs or values. For instance, a manager might pay more attention to a team member's mistakes because they have a preconceived notion that the person is incompetent.
- **Gender Bias:** Making assumptions about abilities, roles, or performance based on someone's gender. This could manifest in assuming a female employee won't be interested in a leadership role or that a male employee won't be as good at empathetic communication.
- **Age Bias:** Judging employees based on their age. This could look like assuming younger employees are not experienced enough for certain tasks or that older employees can't adapt to new technologies.
- **Affinity Bias:** The tendency to get along with others who are like us in some way. In the workplace, this could result in favoring candidates who share the same hobbies, went to the same school, or come from similar backgrounds during hiring or promotions.
- **Halo Effect:** Allowing one positive trait or accomplishment to overshadow other aspects of a person's character or performance. For example, a manager might overlook a team member's poor punctuality because they excel in client interactions.

- **Horns Effect:** The opposite of the halo effect, where one negative trait or mistake colors the perception of all other attributes or actions. An employee who made a significant mistake once might be forever labeled as unreliable.

Acknowledging the existence of these biases is the first step to stopping them from influencing your decisions. From there, it's about actively seeking to view things from different angles, like trying on new glasses to see the world more clearly. Programs offered by organizations like the NeuroLeadership Institute can turn these efforts into a group workout, strengthening your bias-busting muscles.

Tackling internal distractions is a bit like spring cleaning for your mind. Dusting off old thoughts shelves and sorting through the mental clutter allows you to make space for clear, effective communication. The result? A mind that's not just quieter but also a more powerful tool for connecting with others.

Blocking Out the Noise: Managing External Distractions

Speaking of distraction... Let's say you're deep in conversation, trying to hash out the next big idea with your team, and then — BAM! — an email notification pops up. Or maybe it's the relentless construction noise outside. Suddenly, you're not talking about innovative ideas anymore. You're wondering if that email was from the client or just another newsletter. We live in a world filled with distractions. Studies, like one from the University of California, Irvine, show that office workers can expect to be interrupted every 11 minutes. And getting back on track? That takes an average of 23 minutes!

While it's not possible to fight off every single distraction, we combat some external forces that seem bent on derailing our conversations. First things first is taking control of your environment. If you've got an important chat lined up, find a quiet spot. This might mean booking a conference room or finding a cozy corner away from the hustle and bustle.

Technology helps us be more productive and efficient, but it is also one of the most distracting forces in today's world. Tame that tendency by setting some digital ground rules. Before diving into a meeting, why not turn off those pesky notifications? Your email can wait an hour, and so can social media. Even though technology can be a double-edged sword, if you wield it wisely, it becomes your ally. Use apps like 'Freedom' to block distracting websites or apps when you need to focus.

By tackling external distractions head-on, you're not just saving your conversations. You're boosting your overall communication skills. This leads to stronger team bonds, more effective problem-solving, and, let's not forget, a significant uptick in productivity. Whether at work or in our personal lives, mastering the art of blocking out the noise puts you in charge.

However, effective communication isn't solely about overcoming external noise. It also involves tuning into the subtle, nonverbal signals that speak volumes. In the next chapter, you'll learn to do just that.

4

THE SILENT LANGUAGE: DECIPHER NON-VERBAL COMMUNICATION

I've lost count of the number of times I've walked into a room and the vibe just felt off. This has happened to me before anyone has had a chance to say a word. I know I am not unique in having this experience. We have all been in situations where non-verbal communication, the silent orchestra of human interaction, spoke just as loud or even louder than what was said.

Dr. Albert Mehrabian, a pioneer in this field, crunched the numbers and found that 93% of communication effectiveness comes from non-verbal cues—body language, tone of voice, and, yes, even how we dress. Only 7% rely on the actual words we use (MindTools).

Let's say you're chatting with someone who keeps checking their watch or phone. They haven't said a word about needing to be somewhere, but you're getting the hint loud and clear. Or, in a meeting, your boss has crossed arms. His body language gives off the energy that he is closed off or critical, even if he might just be cold or comfortable that way. These non-verbal signals are undercurrents that guide our perceptions and reactions, often without us even realizing it.

Misreading these signals can lead us into choppy waters. Think about it. Just as your boss might be cold and not closed to your input, someone's lack of eye contact might not mean disinterest. They could just be shy. In another instance, someone's gruff tone might not mean they're angry. It could be the culture they grew up in conditioned them to express themselves this way.

Understanding and effectively using non-verbal cues does not mean you have to become a mind reader. More aptly, you must learn to tune into the subtleties of human interaction.

Imagine how much smoother our relationships could be if we paid as much attention to how something is said as to what is said. It could mean the difference between feeling valued and overlooked in the workplace. Personal relationships could mean stronger connections built on empathy and understanding rather than assumptions and misinterpretations.

This chapter is your guide to decoding the silent messages we're all sending and receiving. Sharpening your awareness of non-verbal cues will help you navigate social situations more adeptly, clear up misunderstandings before they escalate, and, ultimately, build deeper, more meaningful relationships.

Body Talk: Deciphering Body Language

Body language is not always the first thing you notice, but it sets the tone and vibe of the conversation. Whether giving a confident thumbs-up or nervously fidgeting with your pen, every gesture, posture, and movement communicates something to the people around you.

Standing tall with your shoulders back and head held high is the universal anthem of confidence. You're silently announcing, "I've got this." On the flip side, slouching is like a visual sigh. It broadcasts feelings of boredom, disinterest, or maybe just having a really long day.

Let's take a closer look at what our body language might be whispering to those around us:

Open Body Language:

- Smiling: "I'm friendly and approachable."
- Uncrossed Arms and Legs: "I'm open to what you say."
- Leaning In: "You've got my full attention and interest."
- Eye Contact: "I respect and am focused on our conversation."

These gestures invite others in, break down barriers, and foster a sense of connection and trust.

Closed Body Language:

- Crossed Arms: "I'm feeling defensive or closed off."
- Avoiding Eye Contact: "I'm nervous, hiding something, or uninterested."
- Tapping Feet or Fingers: "I'm impatient or anxious."
- Turning Away: "I'm trying to distance myself from this conversation."

Closed body language creates walls between people, making creating genuine connections more challenging.

Adapting Your Body Language

Envision that you're at a party. You're scanning the room for a friendly face to chat with. You spot two people — one with arms crossed, leaning back against the wall, and another with a wide smile, hands relaxed at their sides. Who do you approach? Most of us would gravitate towards Mr. or Ms. Open Arms, and that's all thanks to the silent signals of open and closed body language.

Open body language is like a welcome sign hanging on a person's neck. It screams, "Come on over, let's chat!" People with open body language seem more approachable because their posture and gestures invite interaction. They're like human magnets, pulling others into their orbit with ease.

On the flip side, closed body language is the human equivalent of a "Do Not Disturb" sign. It's not always a sign of unfriendliness; sometimes, it's just comfort or self-protection. But to an outsider, it's like a barrier, making it harder for people to feel comfortable approaching.

Understanding these cues can be a game-changer in how we interact. If you're trying to seem more accessible, consciously adopting open body language makes a world of difference. Stand a little more openly, maintain gentle eye contact, and let your arms hang freely or gesture naturally as you talk.

Conversely, suppose you're feeling overwhelmed and need space. In that case, closed body language can be your polite way of saying, "I need a moment." Just be aware of how it's perceived. You don't want to shut someone out accidentally.

So, the next time you're out and about, take a moment to notice your body language and that of those around you. Are you sending out an invite or putting up a wall? Remember, the way we stand, sit, and move can speak volumes before we ever say a word. Body language shapes our social landscapes in ways we might not even realize. Open up, and who knows what conversations and connections await you!

This goes beyond just welcoming others into your personal orbit. Other body language adjustments speak loudly no matter what setting you're in. Aiming to make a killer first impression in a job interview? A firm handshake and direct eye contact say, "I'm competent and confident," before you even introduce yourself. Want to show a friend you're there for them? Open posture and nodding show you're engaged and empathetic.

In essence, becoming fluent in body language allows you to both interpret the silent messages swirling around you and consciously control the signals you're sending out. Ensuring that your verbal communication matches your body language creates the right atmosphere for every interaction.

Face Value: Interpreting Facial Expressions

Facial expressions are the emojis of real life, giving color and context to our words. A smile can be like a warm hug in visual form. It expresses things like "I'm glad to be here" or "I totally agree with you." But just like text messages can be misunderstood without the right emoji, real-life facial cues can also get lost in translation.

For example, you're sharing an idea with a friend, and they respond with furrowed brows. Your first thought might be that they think it's a terrible idea but really, they might just be trying to wrap their head around the concept.

Investing in the art of reading and controlling facial expressions allows you to avoid that confusion more often than not. A simple smile can disarm a tense situation, offering a silent olive branch when words are too clumsy. On the flip side, maintaining a neutral expression, especially during heated discussions, can be like wearing emotional armor, helping you stay composed and keep the conversation from escalating.

Just as you can misinterpret others' facial cues, you must be mindful of what your face tells the world. Ever tried to keep a poker face when you're actually thrilled? It's tough. Our faces can spill our secrets before our lips form the words. That's why becoming aware of your expressions and learning to modulate them is a powerful tool in your communication arsenal.

For example, you might be in a meeting, and the discussion takes a turn that you disagree with. Instead of immediately reacting with a scowl or an eye roll, a controlled, thoughtful expression can give you time to respond diplomatically. It's the equivalent of a mental pause button, giving you a moment to choose your reaction rather than letting your first impulse take the wheel.

Here are more ways you can master your facial cues to steer conversations and impressions:

- **Encouraging Participation:** In a brainstorming session, nodding slightly while maintaining eye contact with speakers can encourage more contributions. It lets the other person know you're listening and that they should keep going without interrupting the flow of ideas.
- **Demonstrating Active Listening:** When someone shares a complex idea or report, tilting your head slightly and furrowing your brows can show you're actively engaged and processing the information. It sends a message of interest and respect for the speaker's effort.
- **Handling Criticism with Grace:** Facing criticism can be tough. Instead of reacting defensively, maintain a calm and neutral expression to help absorb the feedback constructively. Follow up with a thoughtful nod or a small smile to show you're taking the critique seriously, not personally.
- **Conveying Confidence:** Before presenting, take a deep breath and put on a subtle smile. This not only helps calm your nerves but also projects confidence to your audience. A confident stance, complemented by a composed facial expression, makes your words more impactful.
- **Diffusing Tension:** In moments of disagreement or tension, a soft smile paired with a calm demeanor can act as a buffer, reducing the situation's intensity. It's a non-verbal way of saying that you're open to working through the situation together.
- **Expressing Appreciation:** After a team achieves a milestone or someone goes above and beyond, a warm, genuine smile accompanied by direct eye contact can convey your appreciation more deeply than words alone. It's a silent cheer for their hard work and dedication.
- **Showing Openness to New Ideas:** When someone proposes a new idea, raising your eyebrows slightly and nodding shows openness and curiosity, even if you need more convincing. It encourages a culture of innovation and sharing.

Consciously aligning your expressions with your intentions not only enhances your communication skills but also fosters a more positive, collaborative environment. In a nutshell, our faces are the billboards of our emotions, broadcasting our feelings loud and clear. Tuning into the facial expressions of those around us and managing our own make navigating human interactions more graceful with a lot less misunderstanding.

Eye Contact: The Window to the Soul

Eye contact lets you know when you've got a good, strong link with someone else. It's another one of those unspoken things that can say so much without a single word being exchanged. When you lock eyes with someone during a chat, you convey that you're all ears and the other person has your full attention. It's the silent signal of being present, engaged, and genuinely interested in the conversation at hand.

On the other end of the spectrum, dodging eye contact can send sketchy signals, like you're not really into the discussion, hiding something, or just not feeling confident in the moment. It's the equivalent of trying to talk to someone who's constantly looking over your shoulder—pretty off-putting, right?

On the flip side, staring someone down without ever looking away can make the situation just as uncomfortable. Too much eye contact ventures into the "creepy" territory, making people squirm in their seats and pray for a break in the gaze.

You have to find that sweet spot where your eye contact says you're listening and present without tipping into a stare-down contest.

Culture also influences how eye contact is perceived. In some cultures, direct eye contact is a sign of respect and honesty. In others, it's considered too bold or even rude, especially when there's a difference in age or status. Keeping abreast of these cultural nuances ensures you're connecting in a way that respects everyone's comfort zone.

Navigating eye contact in a professional setting, especially in a diverse cultural landscape, can be tricky. Luckily, some universally respectful strategies allow you to use eye contact effectively, ensuring clear and positive communication across any cultural divide:

1. **Start with a Smile:** When initiating eye contact, pair it with a gentle smile. This universal signal of friendliness helps soften the intensity of direct gaze, making the interaction more comfortable for everyone involved.
2. **Use the 50/70 Rule:** Aim to maintain eye contact about 50% of the time while speaking and 70% when listening. This balance keeps the connection engaging without becoming overwhelming.
3. **Practice the Glance-and-Return Technique:** If sustained eye contact is too intense, practice glancing away briefly and returning your gaze. It's like hitting the refresh button—keeping eye contact natural and not too fixed.
4. **Use the Triangle Technique:** To keep eye contact comfortable, imagine a triangle that rotates around the eyes and the bridge of the nose. Shift your focus among these three points gently. It maintains connection without over-staring.
5. **Observe and Adapt:** Pay attention to the other person's comfort level with eye contact. If they frequently look away, they might prefer less directness. Mirror their style to maintain rapport without making them uncomfortable.
6. **Mind Your Blinking:** Blink naturally. Excessive blinking might signal nervousness, while too little can seem overly intense. Natural blinking helps maintain a friendly, open demeanor.
7. **Break It Up in Groups:** When addressing a group, make brief eye contact with different individuals throughout your talk. It creates a sense of inclusion and engagement with everyone present.
8. **Cultural Sensitivity:** Keep in mind that customs vary widely. When in doubt of cultural stances on eye contact, observe

the norms of the host culture or ask a local colleague for advice.
9. **Reflect and Adjust in Real-Time:** Use the immediate feedback you're getting during the interaction to adjust your eye contact—more or less, depending on the reaction you observe.
10. **Practice Makes Perfect:** Like any skill, getting comfortable with eye contact takes practice. Try it out in low-stakes settings to build your confidence.

In the end, eye contact is about building that invisible bridge between you and the person you're talking to. Try to strike a balance that says you're engaged, trustworthy, and confident without overdoing it.

The Power of Touch: Understanding Haptic Communication

At some point, we've all watched a movie scene where two old friends meet after years apart. They rush toward each other and embrace. No words are exchanged, yet you understand perfectly the depth of their bond. That's haptic communication in action—the silent language of touch.

Touches are like stitches that can bind humans together throughout history, conveying comfort, sympathy, or even excitement. Think about the last time someone gave you a pat on the back for a job well done. The touch became a silent cheer that made you feel recognized and appreciated.

Communication through touch taps into a primal part of the human brain, engaging the somatosensory system that processes physical sensations. When we experience a positive touch, such as a hug or a pat on the back, it triggers the release of oxytocin, often dubbed the "love hormone." This hormone plays a huge role in fostering feelings of trust, bonding, and empathy. A surge in its levels lowers cortisol levels, reducing stress and anxiety, and enhances our overall sense of well-being and social connection. The tactile stimulation involved in haptic interactions activates specific brain regions, including the insular cortex, which is involved in emotional and social processing. This neurochemical and neural response underscores the powerful impact of touch on human emotions and relationships, highlighting its special role in communication and social bonding.

Like all other forms of communication, messages can get lost in translation through touch as well. Misinterpretation of touch can lead to awkward mix-ups or discomfort.

When touch is misread, the brain's response shifts dramatically from the positive effects of perceived friendly or comforting touch. Instead of releasing oxytocin, the brain triggers a stress or threat response. This is primarily managed by the amygdala, a region of the brain involved in emotion regulation and perception of fear.

During an uncomfortable or unexpected touch, the amygdala perceives it as a potential threat, activating the body's fight or flight response. This leads to the release of stress hormones like cortisol and adrenaline, preparing the body to either confront the situation or escape from it. This physiological response elevates the heart rate, increases blood pressure, and sharpens the senses, all of which are aimed at ensuring survival in what the brain perceives as a potentially harmful scenario.

Furthermore, the prefrontal cortex, which helps us with decision-making and social behavior, is engaged in an attempt to quickly interpret the touch and its intentions. If the touch is perceived negatively, this area influences feelings of discomfort, violation of personal space, or mistrust towards the initiator.

You can increase the odds of the initiation of a positive response by emphasizing understanding and respecting personal and cultural boundaries. What's considered a warm gesture of friendship in one culture might be seen as too forward or inappropriate in another.

Touch also plays a part in professional settings. A firm handshake, for instance, is universally recognized as a sign of professionalism and confidence. A light, congratulatory pat on the back can also foster a sense of camaraderie and support among team members, as long as it's done with respect and awareness of the other person's comfort level.

The key to mastering haptic communication lies in being attuned to the nuances of touch and the messages they convey within different contexts. It's about striking that delicate balance between connecting genuinely and maintaining professionalism and respect for personal boundaries.

Here are strategies to do just that:

1. **Read the Room:** Always gauge the comfort level of those around you before initiating any form of physical contact. Look for non-verbal cues that might indicate whether a person is open to a handshake, high-five, or a pat on the back.
2. **Start with the Basics:** In professional settings, stick to universally accepted forms of touch like handshakes or, in some cultures, a nod of acknowledgment. These gestures are less likely to be misinterpreted.
3. **Ask for Permission:** When in doubt, especially in more casual or team-building settings, asking for permission before engaging in physical contact ("Is it okay if I give you a high-five?") respects individual boundaries and makes intentions clear.
4. **Respect Declines Gracefully:** If someone seems uncomfortable or declines an offer of physical interaction, respect their choice without taking offense. Their comfort zone differs from yours, and respecting that creates a healthy, inclusive environment.
5. **Reflect on Your Comfort:** Just as you respect others' boundaries, be mindful of your own. You have every right to set limits on physical contact in professional settings, communicating your preferences clearly and respectfully.

Dress to Impress: The Role of Appearance in Non-Verbal Communication

Your outfit is like a book cover. Like it or not, people often read into who you are based on the "cover" you present. Your attire and grooming don't just whisper hints about your personality, profession, and perhaps even your social status. Sometimes, they talk louder than words. Rocking a sharp suit to a job interview? That's like sending a silent handshake that says you mean business and respect this opportunity.

However, just as judging a book by its cover is unfair, it's not cool to box people into stereotypes based solely on their appearance. Yet, it happens. Being mindful of this, you can adjust your outfit so that your style meets the expectations of your professional environment. It's about mastering the art of "dressing to impress" without muffling the essence of who you are. Here are some tips to nail it:

1. **Understand the Dress Code:** Every workplace has one. Whether it's suit-and-tie formal or startup casual, getting a read on the dress code is step one. Like picking the right outfit for the party, you want to fit in, not stick out for the wrong reasons.
2. **Invest in Quality Basics:** Choose a few quality pieces to form the backbone of your wardrobe. Think of a well-fitted blazer, crisp shirt, or sleek trousers. These are your sartorial Swiss Army knives, adaptable and always in style.
3. **Add a Dash of You:** This is where you get to play. A funky tie, an interesting brooch, or a pair of standout shoes can be your nod to personal style without going overboard.
4. **Grooming Matters:** Never underestimate the power of being well-groomed. It's not about vanity. It's about respect—for yourself and for those you interact with. A neat appearance suggests that you're organized and attentive to detail.
5. **Comfort is Key:** If you're uncomfortable in your outfit, it'll show. Comfortable doesn't mean sloppy. It means choosing fabrics and fits that let you move and breathe easily. When

you're comfortable, you're confident, and that's half the battle won.
6. **Adapt and Update:** Styles evolve, and so should your wardrobe. Keeping your professional attire updated (within reason) shows you're in tune with the times. It's like keeping your software updated. It just makes everything run smoother.
7. **Mind the Context:** What works for a creative agency might not fly in a law firm. Tailoring your appearance to the context of your work shows that you respect the norms and expectations of your field.

Dressing for success is a balancing act that melds the expectations of your workplace with your flair. Dressing appropriately sends the right signals, makes positive impressions, and allows you to still feel like yourself. So, go ahead and dress to impress, but remember, the most compelling thing you can wear is your confidence.

The Space Between Us: Understanding Proxemics

I remember being in a few conversations where the other person was so close, I could count their eyelashes. Other times, I've had to practically shout to be heard. We've all been there, right? This relative distance opens up the topic of proxemics—the science of personal bubbles and the invisible lines we draw around us. It's a silent dance we all do, negotiating how close is too close or how far is too far, without ever saying a word.

Your personal space is your invisible comfort zone, a no-entry zone for anyone you're not super cozy with. When someone steps into this zone uninvited, it can feel like an intrusion, like someone barging into your room without knocking. On the flip side, if someone keeps too much distance, you might wonder if they're trying to stay in a different time zone from you.

The amount of space we need varies. The variations stem from a mix of factors:

Cultural Norms

Cultures around the world have different norms when it comes to personal space. For instance, closer physical proximity is common in Mediterranean or Latin American cultures and it signals warmth and friendliness. In contrast, Northern European and many Asian cultures typically prefer more personal space, associating it with respect and personal autonomy. These cultural norms deeply influence individuals' comfort levels and expectations regarding physical distance in social interactions.

Social Relationships

The nature of the relationship between individuals determines comfortable proximity, too. Close friends and family members often interact within a smaller personal space than acquaintances or strangers, as intimacy and trust reduce the need for physical boundaries. Professional relationships, depending on the workplace culture, might require more formal distances to maintain respect and decorum.

Context of Interaction

The setting or context of an interaction also influences personal space preferences. Crowded public spaces like concerts or subways necessitate reduced personal space, which we usually tolerate due to the temporary and impersonal nature of the situation. In contrast, personal or professional meetings in spacious settings may see us instinctively maintaining or even increasing our distance to a more comfortable level.

Individual Preferences

Personal comfort levels with proximity can vary widely even within the same culture or social group. Factors such as personal experiences, upbringing, and even personality traits (e.g., introversion vs. extroversion) influence a person's preferred amount of personal space. Some people feel more secure and focused with a generous bubble of personal space, while others may find closer interactions more engaging and reassuring.

We continuously send and receive nonverbal signals during interactions that we use to unconsciously adjust our sense of needed personal space. Body language, eye contact, and other nonverbal cues invite closer interaction or signal a need for more distance, dynamically shaping the space between us as the conversation progresses.

Gauging what is close enough without being too close means being a bit of a mind reader (without the psychic hotline). You must read these nonverbal cues and adjust on the fly. If you notice someone backing up a bit, don't take it as a personal challenge to close the gap. They're just setting their comfort level. On the other hand, if someone seems to welcome closer proximity, it's likely a sign of trust and rapport.

To use proxemics to your advantage, start by observing. Notice how people cluster at social gatherings, how colleagues interact at work, and even how friends hang out. Pay attention to body language and facial expressions—they're your clues to whether you're in the right spot or if it's time to take a step back (literally).

When in doubt, err on the side of caution and give a little extra space. It's always easier to close a gap than to fix the awkwardness of invading someone's personal bubble.

The Sound of Silence: The Role of Silence in Non-Verbal Communication

Silence, often overlooked, is its own kind of power in communication. It's not just the absence of noise. It's a full-blown statement. A pause charged with meaning. If you were to be sharing your latest idea, and instead of an immediate reaction, you're met with silence. That pause? It's not empty. It's your listener weighing your words, giving them the space they deserve. Silence can be a sign of respect, a moment of contemplation, or a signal that someone is digesting what's been said.

Silence is like a chameleon, changing its colors based on the environment. That same thoughtful pause can easily morph into a cold shoulder if stretched too thin, leaving room for doubt.

"Are they bored? Disappointed? Disagreeing?"

Your mind would race with these types of thoughts if that pause went on longer than a moment, am I right? Without the right cues, silence can quickly be dressed up as disinterest or disapproval, leading us down the path of misunderstandings.

So, how do you harness the power of silence without sending the wrong signals? Here are a few tips:

- **Pair it with Positive Body Language:** A nod or a smile can turn a silence from awkward to affirming, letting the other person know you're engaged and thoughtful, not tuning out.
- **Use it to Listen Actively:** Silence gives others the floor, showing you value their input.
- **Take a Breath Before Responding:** In heated moments, a silent beat allows you to collect your thoughts and respond more calmly. It's a buffer zone, preventing knee-jerk reactions.
- **Signal Before You Dive into Silence:** If you need a moment to think, say so. "Let me take a second to think about that." It frames your silence as purposeful, not dismissive.
- **Reflect and Respect:** Be mindful of how silence is used and received. Some people are more comfortable with silence than others. Pay attention to the other person's comfort with silence and adjust accordingly.

Mastering the art of silence is like fine-tuning an instrument, making it a powerful ally in your communication toolkit. It's about knowing when to pause, when to play, and how to listen to the unspoken.

What's not said is often louder than words. However, the right words at the right time can transform ideas into bridges, connecting minds. Let's explore how that can be done in the next chapter.

5

SPOKEN WORD SYMPHONY - MASTER VERBAL COMMUNICATION

Most of us played the game of telephone in elementary school. Remember how it started with a sentence like "The quick brown fox jumps over the lazy dog" but somehow ended up as "The quick broomsticks over the crazy frog"? In that case, we can clearly see verbal communication gone wrong. Unfortunately, we didn't outgrow that tribulation as we grew up. Verbal communication still gets twisted, but in adulthood, it's not a simple matter of laughing it off like we did back then. Sometimes, one wrong word in the wrong tone at the wrong time leads to frowns, tears, and other stressful outcomes.

But, we can lessen the risk of that being the outcome by being deliberate in how we talk. Don't just open your mouth and let words tumble out when you speak. Rather, craft your message with precision. Take on the outlook that every word matters.

Clarity in speaking cuts through the noise and makes sure your message doesn't just reach the listener's ears but also their understanding. Albert Einstein hit the nail on the head when he said, "If you can't explain it simply, you don't understand it well enough."

Avoid jargon and complex language that could turn your message into a cryptic puzzle.

Clarity isn't just about simplicity, though. It's also about structure. It's an honor for any one of us to listen to a TED Talk by Sir Ken Robinson. His ideas on education aren't just fascinating because of what he says, but how he says it—clear, organized, and irresistibly engaging. Before you speak, take a leaf out of his book. Organize your thoughts to guide your audience through your message without losing them in a maze of tangents.

In a world where a tweet caps at 280 characters, being concise is more than a skill. It's a necessity. Practice distilling your message down to its essence, leaving no room for fluff or confusion. Just like a well-edited tweet can spark a global conversation, a precise message can capture attention and drive your point home.

With verbal communication, remember that clarity, structure, and brevity are your allies. Whether you're presenting in a boardroom, chatting at a networking event, or even making small talk at a dinner party, how you package your message can mean the difference between being heard and being misunderstood. Let's aim for every word to fly straight and true to its target. For that to be your reality, you must first master what your tone conveys while you converse.

Tone Tune-Up: The Influence of Tone in Communication

If you were to listen to your favorite song and it had a completely different beat, it would feel off, right? That's pretty much what happens in communication when the tone doesn't match the message. Your tone—how you say what you say—sets the mood, reinforces the message, and can dramatically alter the listener's response.

Tone conveys the unsaid—the feelings and intentions behind our words. It shapes the context, distinguishing between sarcasm and sincerity, comfort and confrontation. A study in the Journal of Personality and Social Psychology underlines this, showing how the same words, delivered in different tones, can evoke a wide range of emotions in the listener. This is because humans are innately tuned to pick up on vocal nuances as cues to understanding others' states of mind and intentions. Therefore, the tone affects how a message is received and determines the emotional trajectory of a conversation, making it a crucial aspect of effective and empathetic communication.

Consider the scenario of delivering a piece of feedback. Go in with a tone that's too harsh or aggressive, and defenses go up. The message gets lost in the winds of conflict. But approach it with a calm, composed tone, and you're more likely to see understanding and constructive action.

Also, consider if you were to share a funny story and recount it with the enthusiasm of someone reading the phone book, you'll probably hear crickets instead of laughter. But share it with a light, animated tone—picture Jerry Seinfeld in "Comedians in Cars Getting Coffee"—and you bring the story to life, inviting everyone into the joke.

Empathy is a powerful connector, bridging the gap between merely exchanging information and truly understanding and resonating with another person's experiences and emotions. It's a mistake to pigeonhole empathy as a tool only for navigating sad or distressing situations. Empathy shines in all contexts, enabling deeper connection, whether we're sharing in someone's joy, excitement, curiosity, or even their everyday concerns.

The tone of our voice can convey empathy by matching or responding to the emotional state of the person we're communicating with. For example, a warm, enthusiastic tone can amplify someone's excitement about good news, while a soft, gentle tone can offer solace or understanding in more tender moments. Tone allows us to not just share space with someone's feelings but to subtly reflect them, showing that we are truly engaged and present with them.

In her interviews, Oprah Winfrey masterfully uses tone to create a space where guests feel seen, heard, and valued. Her empathetic tone wraps her words in a warm embrace, making even the most guarded guest open up.

You don't have to be a popular TV show host or billionaire to marry tone and empathy well. Whether aiming for calm persuasion in a meeting, sharing a laugh over coffee, or offering a shoulder of support to a friend, tuning up your tone can turn your message from just words into an experience that resonates. Here is how you do that:

- **Match Your Tone to the Situation:** Adapt your tone to fit the context of the conversation. Use a lighter, more upbeat tone for positive news and a softer, more subdued tone for serious discussions.
- **Listen and Reflect:** Pay attention to the tone of the person you're speaking with and gently mirror it. This shows empathy and understanding.
- **Warmth Goes a Long Way:** Regardless of the message, infuse a bit of warmth into your tone to make the conversation feel more inviting and less confrontational.
- **Mind Your Volume:** Adjust your volume to the setting. Speaking too loudly can overwhelm you, while speaking too softly might seem disinterested. Find a comfortable level that invites conversation.
- **Pause for Effect:** Use pauses strategically to let your words sink in or to emphasize certain points. Pauses can also give you a moment to adjust your tone as needed.
- **Be Sympathetic:** Before responding, especially in emotionally charged situations, take a moment to consider the other person's perspective. Let this reflection guide your tone to one of understanding and compassion.
- **Smile, Even on the Phone:** Smiling changes the tone of your voice, making it sound more friendly and open, even if the other person can't see you.
- **Be Genuine:** Authenticity in your tone makes your words more believable and relatable. Avoid a tone that feels forced or insincere. It creates distance rather than connection.
- **Practice Mindfulness:** Being mindful of your emotions and reactions can help you maintain control over your tone,

ensuring it aligns with your intentions and fosters positive interactions.

Listening Ears: The Art of Active Listening

We spend so much time focusing on how to deliver the perfect message we often forget the flip side of the coin: how to be the perfect audience. I have caught myself quietly planning my lunch in my head as another person spoke to me. In that moment, I was not being a very good active listener. Don't be like past me. Luckily, I learned to redirect these wayward thoughts to tuning in, really tuning in, to what's being said to me.

Let me tell you, pausing my thoughts and making space for someone else's used to be hard. So, if you find that you struggle with the task, be gentle with yourself even as you persist. You are part of a large number of us. The fact that you recognize how important it is to do so gives you quite a leg up. A study from Wright State University highlighted that active listening is a hot commodity in the workplace, and it's easy to see why. It gives you the tools to be more understanding, the bridge to honest communication, and the best tool we have to make sure everyone feels heard and valued.

Show the other person that you're truly listening by using non-verbal cues. A nod here, and a smile there sends little signals that say you're present with the other person. Take it from someone like former President Barack Obama, a pro in the communication game. His nods, thoughtful gazes, and smiles don't just make him seem like he's listening. They make people feel listened to.

The buck doesn't stop at understanding active listening. You have to also engage the other party. When you paraphrase what someone's said or toss in a clarifying question, you show that you're paying attention in addition to digging deeper, encouraging the kind of conversation that unfolds ideas and builds connections. Listen to the podcast, "The Joe Rogan Experience," and you will hear active listening in action. Rogan's knack for echoing his guests' thoughts and probing further lights up discussions, making them richer and more nuanced.

By fully engaging with the speaker, using non-verbal cues to show we're tuned in, and responding in ways that deepen the dialogue, we go beyond just hearing. We're actively listening. In doing so, we open up a world where communication flows both ways, leading to more meaningful connections, clearer understanding, and, ultimately, conversations that leave us all feeling a little more seen and a little less alone in this noisy world.

The Power of Pause: Using Silence Effectively in Verbal Communication

Mark Twain wasn't kidding when he pointed out the power of a well-timed pause. It lets your words echo, giving your audience a moment to dive into the pool of your thoughts and swim around before you pull them back to the surface. And when you want to shine a spotlight on something crucial? The silence before you drop your main point can have everyone leaning in, ears perked, ready to catch every word. It's a technique mastered by greats like Martin Luther King Jr., whose strategic silences punctuated his speeches, making his powerful words resonate even more deeply.

While embracing the pause, beware the allure of the dreaded filler words—"um," "like," "you know." These words chip away at the impact of your message, not to mention your perceived confidence. There's a tech fix for that: apps like 'LikeSo' are essentially personal trainers for your speech, helping you catch and cut down on those fillers, clearing the way for your true message to shine.

As we pivot from the nuances of verbal finesse, let's not forget that communication isn't just spoken. It's often written. Mastering Written Communication is our next stop, opening up new dimensions of expression and connection.

You're halfway through "Master Effective Communication," and I'd love to hear your thoughts. Your feedback not only helps me but also others seeking valuable insights.

It's simple to leave a review on Amazon: Visit the book's Amazon 'Write a customer review' page by scanning the code below.

By sharing your experience, you're contributing to a community, helping each other thrive. Your words of wisdom can inspire and guide them, making their journey smoother and more fulfilling.

Your insights matter – thank you for being part of my journey!

6

CRAFTING WORDS THAT RESONATE: CONQUER WRITTEN COMMUNICATION

Since the dawn of civilization, humans have looked for ways to leave their mark, from cave paintings to complex hieroglyphs, leading up to the sophisticated alphabets we use today. This evolution reflects our inherent need to communicate across time and space, making written communication a significant part of human interaction. Fast forward to the present, our ability to articulate thoughts and ideas in writing is more critical than ever, especially in the professional world. Emails, reports, proposals—you name it, each requires a finesse with the written word that can set you apart in your career. In fact, a survey by the National Association of Colleges and Employers highlights written communication skills as a top sought-after attribute in job candidates.

Mastering written communication isn't just about having a way with words. You have to ensure your message is clear, concise, and coherent. Clarity means your grandma and your boss could both grasp your point without a translator. Conciseness is the art of saying what you need without turning your message into "War and Peace." And coherence? It's the golden thread that ties your ideas together so readers don't need breadcrumbs to follow along.

Of course, you have to cross your t's and dot your i's, but great writing involves more than that; it involves a psychological aspect. You need to understand who's on the receiving end of your message. The tone, language, and even the structure of your writing should morph depending on whether you're emailing a coworker about lunch plans or crafting a proposal for your CEO. It's like changing outfits. You wouldn't wear flip-flops to a job interview, and you wouldn't wear a suit to the beach (hopefully). Similarly, adapting your writing style to fit the context and audience means the difference between your message landing like a lead balloon or soaring.

Whether you're jotting down notes, firing off emails, or penning the next great proposal, writing, when executed with skill and sensitivity to your audience, can open doors, illuminate minds, and even change the course of your career.

Improving Your Writing Skills

Boosting your writing skills is a bit like leveling up in a video game: the more quests you undertake (in this case, writing assignments), the better equipped you become to tackle bigger challenges. Here's a cheat code for those looking to sharpen their literary swords:

1. **Practice Makes Perfect:** Just as a musician plays scales to improve, writing regularly hones your ability to communicate clearly and creatively. Every word you write builds your skill, whether it's daily journaling, blogging, or drafting memos.
2. **Be a Bookworm:** Diving into books, articles, or social media posts expands your understanding of different writing styles and vocabularies. Notice what captures your attention and why. Is it the writer's humor, their concise way of making a point, or how they turn a phrase? Mix and match these elements in your writing to discover what works best for you.
3. **Embrace Technology:** Tools like Grammarly are like the helpful sidekick in your writing adventures, pointing out the pitfalls (grammar mistakes) and monsters (punctuation

errors) lurking in your drafts. They're a great way to learn from your mistakes and avoid them in the future.
4. **Seek Out Your Sensei**: Feedback is the dojo for your writing skills. A fresh set of eyes can catch things you've missed and provide insights you hadn't considered. That trusted colleague can be your sparring partner, helping you refine your message before it reaches the wider world.
5. **Never Stop Learning**: The quest for writing excellence is never-ending. Resources abound for those willing to seek them out—online courses that challenge you to write better, books that delve into the craft (William Zinsser's "On Writing Well" is the equivalent of a legendary sword for your arsenal), and workshops that offer personalized guidance.

Adapting Your Writing for Different Contexts

Chameleons are admired for blending into different environments with ease. You can learn a thing or two from them because that's how you should approach writing in various contexts. Your words, tone, and style need to shift to match the setting and audience, just like a chameleon changes its colors.

For instance, shooting off an email to a coworker? Because of the relationship you built with this person, it might feel like you're grabbing coffee with a friend. Keep it light and informal. Maybe even crack a joke or two. But drafting a report for your boss is another ball game. It's like presenting at a conference. You'd want your suit pressed and your points polished, formal, and precise, ensuring every word earns its place on the page.

Suppose you're putting together a proposal for a new project. In that case, you need to be the Shakespeare of clarity and the Einstein of persuasion, highlighting the whys and hows, making benefits shine and concerns vanish. The true power of the written word lies not just in its ability to inform or persuade but in its capacity to stir emotions and galvanize action. Writing transforms from mere text on a page to a catalyst that moves people, drives change, and creates impact when exerted with skill.

Consider the impassioned plea of a nonprofit organization, reaching out through a heartfelt letter that paints a vivid picture of the cause they champion. It's not merely a request for donations. In that context, it's an invitation to be part of something greater, to join a community of change-makers. The stories shared, the struggles highlighted, and the vision for the future are all carefully crafted to tug at the heartstrings, igniting a sense of urgency and empathy that transcends the physical distance between the reader and the cause.

Similarly, think about an entrepreneur pitching an innovative idea through a carefully composed email or business plan. The goal isn't just to list features and benefits but to imbue the reader with a sense of excitement and possibility. The narrative aims to spark the imagination, painting a picture of a future made better by this innovation. If the reader feels the potential impact on a personal level, they are driven to invest, support, or join in.

Even in everyday contexts, the emotional pull of the written word can inspire action. A well-crafted apology can mend fences, conveying genuine remorse and the promise of change. An uplifting message can bolster a friend's spirits, offering solace and motivation during tough times. In each instance, it's the emotional resonance of the writing that transforms static words into dynamic forces of human connection and action. To have as powerful an impact:

1. **Tap into Emotions:** Use vivid imagery and sensory details to create a strong emotional connection with your readers. Paint a picture that allows them to see, feel, and experience the situation or idea you're presenting.
2. **Tell a Story:** Everyone loves a good story. When appropriate, incorporate personal anecdotes or hypothetical scenarios that relate to your main point. Stories humanize your message and make complex ideas more relatable and memorable.

3. **Use Powerful Words:** Choose words that pack an emotional punch. Words like "transform," "revolutionize," "empower," and "overcome" can inspire and motivate readers to take action.
4. **Connect With Your Audience:** Tailor your message to resonate with your specific audience. Understand their hopes, fears, and dreams, and align your message with what matters most to them.
5. **Call to Action:** End with a clear, compelling call to action. Be specific about what you want your readers to do next. A direct appeal gives your emotionally charged message a clear direction, turning inspiration into action.

Remember, every email you send, report you write, and proposal you craft are all reflections of you. A poorly constructed message sends the wrong signals. But get it right? You'll not only look good, but you'll boost your professional cred, making people sit up and take notice.

The Role of Technology in Written Communication

In this digital age, our thumbs do a lot of talking, and a single email can cross continents faster than a plane. It's a world where over 300 billion emails zip around the globe daily (Statista, 2023). These are such a hallmark in modern professional writing that you must invest in making your best impression no matter the platform you use to type up these messages. Here are some tips to ensure your emails get read and leave a positive impression:

1. **Subject Line Precision:** Treat the subject line as your headline. Make it specific and compelling to grab attention. A clear subject line sets the expectation and helps recipients prioritize their inboxes.
2. **Get to the Point:** Time is precious. Start with a brief greeting, then dive straight into the purpose of your email.

Whether it's a request, an update, or a response, clarity, and brevity are your best friends.
3. **Structure for Success**: Break your email into short paragraphs, each with a clear point. Use bullet points or numbered lists to make your email easier to scan. This structure helps recipients quickly grasp your message.
4. **Polish Your Tone**: Aim for a professional yet approachable tone. It's a fine line between being overly formal and too casual. When in doubt, err on the side of formality, but don't be afraid to add a touch of warmth or personality where appropriate.
5. **Call to Action**: Be clear about what you want the recipient to do next. Whether it's replying by a certain date, providing information, or taking a specific action, your call to action should be unmistakable.
6. **Sign Off with Style**: End your email with a courteous sign-off, such as "Best regards," "Sincerely," or "Thank you," followed by your name. A professional signature with your contact information adds a polished touch.
7. **Consider the Timing**: Timing can impact how your email is received. Avoid sending non-urgent emails late at night or on weekends, unless that's the norm in your industry or company.
8. **Use 'Reply All' Sparingly**: Before hitting 'Reply All,' consider whether everyone on the thread needs to see your response. Overuse can clutter inboxes and dilute your message's effectiveness.
9. **Attachments and Links**: If you're including attachments or links, mention them in the body of your email to ensure they don't go overlooked. Make sure attachments are appropriately sized and formatted for easy access.

Mastering email etiquette tips makes every email an opportunity to reinforce your professionalism and enhance your working relationships.

In addition to emails, countless instant messages and social media posts pile up in modern communication. This digital revolution has transformed the way we write, turning screens into our paper and keyboards into our pens.

The beauty of technology is that it's not just a medium for our messages. It's also a tool to polish them. Ever felt like grammar was a maze with no exit? Cue tools like Grammarly and Hemingway Editor, acting like digital breadcrumbs leading you out of the woods, ensuring your writing is as clear and sharp as a samurai sword. And then there's the organizational wizardry of email platforms, with features that let you schedule emails to hit just at the right moment or set reminders so that no message ever falls into the black hole of your inbox.

But, as with all great powers, there's a catch. The screen that connects us also conceals us, stripping away the nuances of face-to-face interaction and leaving room for misinterpretation. Luckily, emojis and GIFs act as the cavalry of digital communication, charging in to add a splash of emotion and clarify your tone, turning what could be seen as snark into the sarcasm it was meant to be.

Using this digital landscape necessitates that we use our tools wisely, balancing clarity with personality, and remembering that behind every screen is a human, just like us. Embracing the role of technology in written communication closes the gap between the coldness of the keyboard and the warmth of human connection, ensuring our messages reach their destination and truly resonate.

Write and Wrong: Common Mistakes and How to Avoid Them

When writing, one wrong word gets your message lost in a cloud of confusion. But, by spotting these common pitfalls, you can keep your writing clear, credible, and compelling. Let's break down some classic blunders and how to dodge them:

1. **The Jargon Jungle:** Ever read something so crammed with technical gibberish that you need a decoder ring? That's the

jargon trap. Sticking to plain language boosts understanding and keeps your audience engaged. So, before you type out "utilize," ask yourself if "use" would do the trick. The goal is to communicate, not complicate.
2. **The Proofreading Pitfall:** A typo can be a distraction at best and a detriment to your credibility at worst. A Grammarly survey in 2020 found that 59% of people would think twice about buying from a brand that blasts out content peppered with typos or grammar blunders (Grammarly, 2022). The fix? Take the time to read over your work. Apps like Grammarly can be a second set of eyes, catching those sneaky errors before they go public.
3. **The Vagueness Vortex:** Being vague in your writing does not lead to a powerful drive to action. Instead of saying "soon" or "a lot," pin down the specifics. Will the project be done by Thursday? How many are "a lot"? Numbers, dates, and concrete details clear the fog, ensuring everyone's on the same page.

Writing is less about impressing with fancy words and more about connecting, informing, and persuading. The pen (or keyboard) is mightier than the sword, especially when executed with precision and care. But that is only the case if you're confident enough to use it properly. Let's discuss that next.

7

BOOSTING YOUR SELF-BELIEF: THE CONFIDENCE CONNECTION

What if you stepped onto a stage? Imagine this scenario with me. The spotlight hits, and all eyes are on you. Do you experience that flutter in your stomach? I am well familiar with that feeling when nerves meet excitement, and the odds are that you are, too. You could crumble under the weight of the scrutiny or you could use this knee-knocking moment as your time to shine. Confidence is what allows you to take advantage of the latter option. It is what will allow you to own the stage and achieve your objective, whether it is to entertain, inspire, or educate. Confidence transforms good communicators into great ones. It's the difference between mumbling through your presentation and owning the room.

Albert Bandura, a giant in the world of psychology, highlights the concept of self-efficacy—basically, believing in your abilities. Self-efficacy is another word for self-confidence. When it comes to chatting, presenting, or even negotiating, believing you've got what it takes is half the battle. I am not preaching just motivational poster stuff to you. Research from the University of Nebraska-Lincoln backs it up, showing that folks with a hearty dose of self-confidence come across as more persuasive and credible.

Confidence doesn't just amp up what you say. It supercharges how you say it. When someone speaks with assurance, their voice becomes steady and strong while their posture makes them seem like they're rooted to the spot—not stiff, but powerful. Confident people not only talk the talk but they walk the walk. Their body language sings the same tune as their words, making their aura irresistibly convincing.

When using words themselves, confident communicators know how to use just the right vocabulary. The Society for Personality and Social Psychology found that a sprinkle of self-assurance can lead to a richer, more varied use of language, giving your communication that extra sparkle.

Even if your confidence levels are low right now, this is a skill that you can beef up. Anyone can increase self-confidence. But don't expect a miraculous change. More realistically, these changes will be incremental but powerful. Becoming more confident is a journey, not a sprint. It's about accumulating experiences that reinforce your belief in your ability to express yourself. With every word you speak and gesture, you're not just communicating with others. You're telling yourself that you've got this. And before you know it, you'll not only believe it but also live it, making every stage, meeting room, or dinner table your moment to shine.

Strategies to Boost Your Confidence

Boosting your confidence builds a sturdy foundation of belief in yourself, especially when it comes to communicating. Here's how to make your confidence soar:

Start with a Pep Talk

We're often our own harshest critics. Flip that script! Feed your mind positive affirmations so you can turn into your loudest cheerleader instead. Instead of letting the "I can'ts" and "I'm not good enoughs" take center stage, start telling yourself, "I've got this," and "I'm a great communicator." It might feel odd at first, but a study in the Journal of

Personality and Social Psychology confirms that positive self-talk leads to a rise in self-confidence.

Practice, Practice, Practice

There's no way around it. Becoming a better communicator is all about putting in the work. Like learning any other skill, such as playing an instrument or mastering a new language, the more you do it, the better you get. Terrified of public speaking? Joining a group like Toastmasters to dispel the belief that this is something you can't do. You can do it, and that is something you prove to yourself the more you do it. Toastmasters is a space where stumbles are part of the process, and every speech is a step toward becoming more poised and self-assured.

See It to Be It

Let's talk about visualization. There is a myth that this practice is equivalent to daydreaming your way to success—a nice vision but something that does not achieve real results. The truth is that this is a legit tool used by top performers in all fields around the world. Picture yourself nailing that presentation, wowing the crowd, or having a conversation where every word lands just right. Michael Phelps, a swimming legend, visualized every race down to the stroke. This mental rehearsal primes your brain to act confidently because, in a way, it's been there before.

Overcoming Communication Anxiety

If the thought of speaking up feels like you're about to leap out of a plane without a parachute rather than just a case of nerves, you may be suffering from communication anxiety. It's a common affliction affecting many, especially when stepping into unfamiliar territory or the stakes are high. Feeling those butterflies isn't your enemy, though. It just makes you human. Dr. David Carbonell, a clinical psychologist specializing in anxiety management, tells us that the key to overcoming this anxiety is doing the opposite of what you'd instinctively do. Instead of fighting that anxiety, give it a nod. Recognize it, tip your hat to it, and invite it to sit down. Then, you can focus on turning down the volume on that anxiety.

Let's say you're moments away from delivering a speech. Your heart's racing, and your palms are sweaty—classic Eminem moment. This is when you do the 4-7-8 breathing technique. Inhale slowly for four counts, hold that breath for seven, and then let it all out for eight. It's as simple as that, but the effect is huge. You've effectively taken control of your nervous system, shifting you from panic mode to chill mode.

Suppose you still find that anxiety hangs around and turns every speaking opportunity into a nightmare. In that case, it might be time to call in the pros. Cognitive-behavioral therapy (CBT) can help you. It's got a solid track record for helping folks untangle the knots of anxiety, teaching you to challenge those doom-filled thoughts and replace them with a can-do attitude.

It's okay to be anxious. There are tools and techniques out there to help you face it head-on. These mentioned are just a sample of what is available to you. So, next time you feel that familiar flutter, remember: you've got this. Embrace it and breathe through it. Every great communicator started somewhere. You'll find your voice with a bit of courage, too.

Cultivating Confidence Through Personal Growth

Confidence is like a plant. Just as a plant needs water, sunlight, and a bit of TLC to flourish, your confidence thrives on a mix of requirements. The first is lifelong learning. Making it a priority to continuously educate yourself opens up a treasure chest of knowledge and skills, making you not just more knowledgeable but also surer of your footing in any conversation. Platforms like Coursera and Udemy are like greenhouses for your confidence plant, offering sunlight in the form of courses that range from improving your communication skills to mastering public speaking.

MASTER EFFECTIVE COMMUNICATION

...nk about the last time you nailed something, big or small. Maybe ...as getting through a tough talk without the conversation derail... ...or perhaps it was a presentation that landed just right. Cele-...ng these moments isn't just about giving yourself a pat on the ... Acknowledging these achievements is another element that ...ases confidence by nourishing your self-belief and keeping you ...vated.

...ience—the ability to spring back after a setback—is the final ...th component we will discuss in this section. It's the strong root ...m that keeps your confidence plant standing tall, even when ...e and rejection try to knock it down. Embracing a growth mind-... Dr. Carol Dweck, psychologist, suggests, means viewing every ...ble as a step and every challenge as a chance to grow. This ...set doesn't just protect your self-esteem. It turns it into a well-... of confidence.

...u nurture your confidence through learning, celebrating, and ...ing back, you'll find it becomes easier to stand tall and share ...houghts, your ideas, and your story. With such confidence, you ...ptivate any audience, turning presentations into conversations ...teners into participants. In the next chapter, let's dive into how ...ture an audience's attention, leveraging your confidence to ...nd truly connect.

8

COMMANDING THE ROOM: THE ROADMAP TO RIVETING PRESENTATIONS

Delivering an engaging presentation is more than just standing up and talking in front of a crowd. For the impact of your word to hit and ripple through the minds of the people listening, you need to make a real connection with your audience. The great news is that you don't have to reinvent the wheel to do this. An engaging presentation has a certain look and feel to it – an anatomy, if you will. Once you can recreate these parts, your points are as good as sold to the listeners.

Engaging presentations have the right blend of these three components:

1. Content
2. Delivery
3. Audience engagement

Let's talk some more about each of these features.

The content you present should be crystal clear, concise, and relevant to your audience. Take a look at Simon Sinek's TED talk called "Start With Why." He delivers a message that is straightforward and to the point, and it resonates deeply with the audience. That's the power of clear and concise content. You can construct impactful content too. Here's how:

- **Know Your Audience:** Take the time to understand who your audience is, what their needs and interests are, and what information they are looking for. Think about Steve Jobs when he introduced the iPhone at the 2007 Macworld conference. He knew his audience consisted of tech enthusiasts who were eager for innovative products. By understanding his audience's expectations and interests, he tailored his presentation to captivate and excite them.
- **Define Your Key Message:** Before creating your content, clearly define the key message you want to convey. This will help you stay focused and ensure that your content is concise and to the point. Your message should be clear and easily understandable so that your audience can grasp it quickly.
- **Use Plain Language:** Avoid using jargon, technical terms, or complex language that may confuse or alienate your audience. Bill Gates is a smart guy with a huge vocabulary. However, when he talks about public health, he breaks down complex concepts into simple, understandable language, making it accessible to a wide range of people. Speaking your audience's language helps them connect with your message and makes it easier for them to follow along.
- **Organize Your Content:** Structure your content in a logical and organized manner. Use headings, subheadings, and bullet points to break down information into manageable chunks. This will make it easier for your audience to follow along and grasp the main points of your content.
- **Provide Examples and Visuals:** Use relevant examples and visuals, such as images, charts, or graphs, to support your main points and make your content more engaging. Visual aids can help clarify complex concepts, make information

more memorable, and capture your audience's attention. More on this soon!

With your content created, you must then deliver it. How you do so controls how your message is received. Think about Tony Robbins, a well-known motivational speaker. This dynamic and energetic delivery style keeps his audience engaged and captivated. The way he uses his tone, body language, and pacing adds an extra layer of impact to his message. So, remember, how you deliver your presentation matters just as much as what you say.

Your delivery style might differ from Tony's, but some universal truths apply to delivering engaging presentations:

- **Start with a Bang:** Begin your presentation with a compelling opening that grabs your audience's attention. You can use a thought-provoking question, a surprising fact, or a captivating story to engage your listeners immediately.
- **Tell Stories:** Share relevant and relatable stories that illustrate your main points. Stories captivate an audience, evoke emotions, and make your message more memorable.
- **Be Enthusiastic:** Show enthusiasm and passion for your topic. Your energy will be contagious, and it will help keep your audience engaged and interested. Use varied vocal tones, gestures, and body language to convey excitement and keep the energy levels high.
- **Address the Needs and Concerns:** Acknowledging your audience's concerns or challenges shows that you understand them and are there to provide valuable insights. In Brene Brown's TED talk on vulnerability, she addressed common human emotions and experiences, making her talk relatable to a wide audience. By addressing their needs and concerns, you create a sense of relevance and establish a bond with your listeners. A Q&A session is the perfect time to do this. We will discuss how to handle that soon.

This also ties into delivery, and that encourages interaction with your audience. Create opportunities for audience participation and interaction. Ask questions, encourage discussions, or even use interactive activities to involve your listeners. When the audience feels involved, they become active participants rather than passive observers, making the presentation more engaging. Look at Oprah Winfrey as an example. She is a master at creating a dialogue with her audience. She makes them feel like they are part of the conversation, and that connection is what makes her presentations truly engaging

Commanding the room might seem like something that is out of your reach now but that is anxiety talking. If that is the case, the first order of business is to confront that voice.

Facing the Fear: Tackling Stage Fright

We've all had to speak in front of the class in school and for most of us, it was no fun. Even waiting for your turn can feel like agony.

Heart pounding.

Sweaty palms.

A knot in your stomach, causing butterflies to flutter around.

Shallow and fast breathing.

I can go on and on about the physical expressions, and they all boil down to being the victim of stage fright, also known as performance anxiety. While it manifests differently for everyone, there are some common feelings and sensations associated with it. Negative thoughts are another one of these, telling you that you're not good enough... That you'll embarrass yourself in front of everyone.

The mix of anxiety, nervousness, and fear can be quite overwhelming. Don't get down on yourself if you relate to this. Many people experience stage fright, including experienced performers and public speakers. It's a natural response to the pressure and visibility of being on stage.

The good news is that these feelings can be reduced, and stage fright can be overcome. The first thing that needs to be done is understanding the root of your fear. It could be fear of being judged by others, fear of forgetting your lines, or fear of being in the spotlight. Take Richard Branson, for example. Despite being a successful entrepreneur, he openly discusses his fear of public speaking. Acknowledging his fear and confronting it head-on allows him to manage and overcome it.

Follow up self-awareness with preparation. Knowing your content inside out boosts your confidence and reduces anxiety. Look at Susan Cain, the author of "Quiet: The Power of Introverts in a World That Can't Stop Talking." She spent a whole year preparing for her TED talk, which has now become one of the most viewed talks of all time. Her dedication to preparation allowed her to deliver a powerful and confident presentation. You can do the same by investing time in practicing and becoming an expert on your subject matter.

Practice makes perfect! The more you expose yourself to public speaking, the more comfortable you will become over time. In addition to possibly joining a local Toastmasters club to practice speaking in a supportive and encouraging environment, try rehearsing your presentation in front of friends or family. Their feedback and encouragement might boost your confidence and help you build resilience against stage fright.

Tackling stage fright is a journey. Each small step you take by exposing yourself to public speaking makes you a confident and engaging speaker. Don't let fear hold you back—step onto that stage and share your voice with the world.

Powerful Visual Aids: More Than Just Pretty Pictures

Visual aids should enhance your presentation by adding visual interest, reinforcing your message, and helping your audience understand your content better. Make the most of visual aids by:

Keeping It Simple

Complex or cluttered visuals can confuse your audience and distract them from your message. Edward Tufte is a pioneer in data visualization. He emphasizes the importance of simplicity, clarity, and meaningful visuals. Aim for clean and straightforward visuals that convey your message effectively without overwhelming your audience with unnecessary complexity.

Using Visuals to Reinforce, Not Repeat, Your Message

Visual aids should compliment your spoken words and provide additional value to your presentation. When Al Gore presented "An Inconvenient Truth," he used visuals that reinforced his message about climate change. His visuals – graphs and images – helped his audience grasp the magnitude of the issue and understand the data compellingly. Think about how you can use visuals to enhance and emphasize your key points, rather than duplicating what you're already saying.

Ensuring Your Visuals Are Accessible to All Audience Members

Accessibility is important and your visual aids should be designed with inclusivity in mind. Consider color contrast for those with visual impairments, so that everyone can easily see and understand your visuals. Additionally, provide alternative text or descriptions for those who may not be able to see the visuals, ensuring they can still follow along and comprehend the content. The Web Accessibility Initiative offers guidelines for creating accessible presentations that consider the needs of all audience members.

Mastering Q&A Sessions

Handling questions from the audience can be challenging, but with the right strategies, you can turn it into an opportunity to engage your audience further and reinforce your message. Here's how you can excel in Q&A sessions:

Anticipate Possible Questions

You need to play the role of a mind reader with this. Put yourself in your audience's shoes and envision the questions that might arise based on your presentation. Follow in the footsteps of TED speakers, who meticulously prepare for potential post-talk questions. By doing so, you'll be armed with thoughtful responses and an air of confidence.

Listen Attentively

When a question is fired your way, take a moment to truly absorb it and craft your response. Allow a pregnant pause to hang in the air, signifying that you value the question and are giving it the careful consideration it deserves. This brief interlude allows you to concoct a well-constructed answer that hits the bullseye.

Treat Each Question as An Opportunity to Reinforce Your Key Points

Keep your compass pointed in the direction of your main message and use the queries as stepping stones to drive it home. Just like Sheryl Sandberg, who skillfully used a question about work-life balance to underscore her advocacy for gender equality in the workplace, you can weave your responses into the fabric of your central theme.

Embrace The Art of Brevity

Long-winded answers can transform a captivating Q&A session into a tedious monologue. Take inspiration from former US president Bill Clinton, renowned for providing concise yet comprehensive answers. By keeping your responses succinct and laser-focused, you'll maintain the audience's undivided attention and leave a lasting impact.

The Art of Storytelling in Presentations

In the professional setting, there's often an unspoken expectation to maintain a certain level of distance from our colleagues and clients. However, delivering a good presentation necessitates prioritizing and fostering that human connection. There's no better way to achieve this than through the art of storytelling.

Stories bridge the gap between individuals, transcend formalities, and create a shared experience. It allows us to tap into our shared humanity to capture attention, spark emotions, and build a genuine connection with our audience. By weaving narratives into our presentations, we break down barriers, invite empathy, and leave a lasting impact.

Here's how you can harness the magic of storytelling:

Embrace The Strength of Personal Stories

Share your own experiences to infuse your presentation with authenticity and relatability. In J.K. Rowling's Harvard commencement speech, she shared personal stories that struck a chord with the audience, reminding them of the power of resilience and imagination.

Construct A Narrative Structure for Your Presentation

Just like a good story, your presentation should have a clear beginning, middle, and end. Frame your content as a story, with a defined problem at the beginning, a solution in the middle, and a compelling outcome at the end. This narrative structure helps your audience follow along and engage with your message.

Employ Storytelling Techniques to Bring Your Presentation Alive

Use vivid language that paints a picture in the minds of your listeners. Create suspense by building anticipation and gradually revealing key information. And don't be afraid to evoke emotions that resonate with your audience. Martin Luther King Jr.'s iconic "I Have a Dream" speech was skillfully fortified with vivid language and emotional appeal to convey his message of equality and justice.

Storytelling is such a masterful aspect of not only presentation but communication as a whole. Turn to the next chapter where we will dive deeper into how to employ its power.

9

UNLEASH THE POWER OF STORYTELLING IN COMMUNICATION

Ever wonder why some movies or books leave you feeling like you've just feasted on a gourmet meal while indulging others feel like you've been left with an empty plate? It's not about flashy special effects, big-name stars, or even a hefty marketing budget. The secret ingredient is good old-fashioned storytelling. There's a pulse to stories that resonate with us...a series of beats that, when hit just right, pulls us deep into the world of the narrative, making us laugh, cry, or sit on the edge of our seats in suspense.

Utilizing the magic of storytelling isn't just for authors or filmmakers. It is a skill that can transform anyone's communication game. Picture sitting around a campfire, the flames flickering and casting shadows, as someone begins to tell a story. Without even realizing it, you're hooked, hanging on every word. Why? Because stories have the unique ability to transport us to a space in time and make facts and figures breathe and dance. According to research from the London School of Business, while we might only remember a measly 5% to 10% of dry statistics, throw those facts into a story, and suddenly up to 70% of that information sticks. Think about any TED Talks that have stayed with you. Chances are, the speaker told a tale that made you see the world a little differently.

But stories do more than just entertain or educate. They persuade by making heartfelt connections. Neuroeconomist Paul Zak discovered that a good story gets our brains to release oxytocin, which makes us feel all warm and connected to the storyteller and their tale. This isn't just cool science trivia. It's a key to unlocking deeper engagement, whether you're presenting in a boardroom or chatting at the water cooler. If you've ever tried to get your team excited about a new project, you know this can be difficult. You could bombard them with charts and bullet points, yes, and have to ensure the barely veiled yawns and distracted gazes. Or you could share a story about someone whose life was changed by what you're working on. Suddenly, your project isn't just another item on their to-do list. It's a quest, a shared journey in which they're emotionally invested.

Storytelling is versatile. It can be tied into any form of communication, from a pitch to an email, making your message heard, felt and remembered. By telling stories, you're inviting your audience into a world where they can see, feel, and believe in your message as deeply as you do.

Crafting Your Story: The Essential Elements

Good stories follow a rhythm that we're all subconsciously familiar with, thanks to centuries of human storytelling. The stories that suck us in and refuse to let go are those that follow a certain sequence of events or beats. These beats are the milestones of our journey through the story, guiding us like a map.

When a story misses these beats, or hits them out of order, it's like listening to a song where the notes are off—it just doesn't feel right. Our brains crave this narrative structure. It's how we make sense of the stories we're told. That's why, when a book or movie ends and we're left feeling underwhelmed, it's often because the story didn't follow the beat.

This doesn't just apply to what we see as traditional forms of stories like books and films. It applies in professional lives, too. Our personal lives too when you think about it. Every good story needs a clear structure:

1. A beginning that draws you in
2. A middle that escalates the drama
3. An end that ties all loose ends, leaving you satisfied yet longing for more.

Take the following email circulated through a fashion business as an example of this story structure in action:

Subject: The Journey of Our Fall Collection: From Concept to Catwalk

Dear Team,

I hope this message finds you well and brimming with creativity. As we stand on the cusp of launching our Fall Collection, I wanted to take a moment to share the story behind it—a journey that each of you has played a vital role in.

The Beginning: A Spark of Inspiration

Our journey began in the bustling streets of Paris, where a chance encounter with a vintage fashion exhibit sparked the idea that would become the heart of our collection. Inspired by the timeless elegance and bold expressions of the past, we set out to blend tradition with innovation. This was no small feat, but I knew we had the talent and determination to make it happen.

The Middle: Overcoming Challenges Together

As with any great endeavor, our path was lined with challenges. Fabric shortages threatened our timelines, and design disagreements tested our resolve. Yet, it was in these moments that our team truly shined. Remember the late nights spent brainstorming over cups of coffee, and the weekend we all chipped in to hand-finish the prototype designs? Each obstacle was met with unwavering resolve and a shared commitment to our vision.

The End: A Triumph Shared

And now, as our collection is about to debut on the catwalk, we have more than just stunning designs to celebrate. We have the story of us—a tale of collaboration, perseverance, and the shared joy of creation. This collection is a testament to what we can achieve together, and each piece carries the imprint of our collective spirit.

As we move forward, let's carry the lessons and bonds forged in this journey into our next projects. I am incredibly proud of what we have accomplished and even more excited about what the future holds.

Thank you for your hard work, your passion, and your belief in what we do. Here's to our continued success and the many stories we have yet to tell.

Warmest regards,

[Name]

This narrative arc is the backbone of storytelling that keeps listeners leaning in closer, eager to hear what happens next.

What's a story without its heroes and villains? Characters are the heart and soul of any tale. They're the ones we root for, the ones we love to hate, and the ones we see ourselves in. Let's say you're at work, introducing a new initiative. Ditch the PowerPoint slides filled with bullet points for a moment and talk about the people behind the project—the passionate team leader, the tech whiz who solved a problem at the eleventh hour, or the intern who came up with a game-changing idea. Watch how the project is altered from a list of objectives to a human story that is relatable and riveting.

Conflict and resolution are what keep us on the edge of our seats with a story. You don't have to create unnecessary drama but instead highlight the challenges faced and overcome. In a business context, sharing a story of a challenge your team faced, the hurdles you encountered, and how you triumphed in the end isn't just informative. It's inspiring as shown by the example above. It transforms your words into a journey, with highs and lows that everyone can rally behind, fostering a deeper connection and sense of achievement among your colleagues.

Crafting your story with these essential elements in mind—structure, characters, and conflict—turns a simple narrative into an engaging, memorable experience. Whether you're sharing a personal anecdote, pitching an idea, or rallying your team around a cause, remember that at the heart of every great story is the ability to connect, engage, and inspire.

Storytelling Techniques for Effective Communication

Having the foundations, walls, and roof up does not make a house a home. In the same way, your story is not complete because the structure is nailed down. There are other elements needed to ensure it draws your audience in. The great news is that you don't need to be a literary genius to do it. To create a story that sticks, consider using these devices:

Metaphors and Analogies

Metaphors are figures of speech that describe something by comparing it to something else, without using "like" or "as," to highlight similarities in a creative or thought-provoking way. For example, saying "time is a thief" suggests that time steals moments from us, without directly stating it.

Analogies, on the other hand, draw a comparison between two different things to explain a concept or idea by highlighting their similarities, often using "like" or "as." For instance, explaining electricity flow through wires by comparing it to water flowing through pipes makes the concept easier to understand by relating it to a familiar experience.

Metaphors and analogies both take something unfamiliar and explain it in terms everyone can grasp. In our professional worlds, using them can transform complex, abstract ideas into relatable, understandable concepts. By likening a complicated business strategy to a game of chess, for instance, you immediately provide a clear, vivid understanding of the strategy's intricacies, making your audience more likely to grasp and remember your message. This approach not only aids comprehension but also engages the audience's imagination, making your communication more effective and memorable. At the 2017 Google I/O, Sundar Pichai explained AI by comparing it to a child learning to tell dogs from cats. Suddenly, AI isn't this nebulous, techy thing—it could be seen as natural as growing up. When using metaphors, pick something universally understood. Like comparing a complex problem-solving process to solving a jigsaw puzzle—it instantly paints a picture in your audience's mind.

Personal Anecdotes

Sharing a slice of your life can turn a presentation from a monologue into a dialogue, building a bridge between you and your audience. Sheryl Sandberg's book "Lean In" is packed with personal stories that transform her from a Silicon Valley exec to someone you might chat with over coffee.

You can't throw in just any personal tale. The key to picking the right anecdotes is relevance. Your story should mirror the emotions or situations your audience might face to make your message not just heard but felt. Think about a time you faced a challenge or a moment of failure that taught you a lesson. These stories resonate because they're real and relatable.

Creating Suspense and Surprise

Everyone loves a good plot twist. It's what keeps us glued to our seats in a movie theater. TED speakers like Sir Ken Robinson and Brené Brown are masters of this, leading you down a path and then—bam—hitting you with a surprise that flips everything on its head. To create suspense, start by posing a question or presenting a problem that seems insurmountable. Then, guide your audience through the twists and turns of your thinking process, keeping the solution just out of reach until the perfect moment. The reveal should be something unexpected yet inevitable, leaving your audience with a satisfying "aha!" moment that they'll remember long after.

Have a hard time imagining how this plays out? Look at this example for inspiration. In a corporate team meeting, a project manager introduces a complex new project management software.

She begins, "Imagine we're about to climb Mount Everest, but instead of heavy backpacks and physical strain, our challenge lies in navigating the maze of our current project tasks, deadlines, and communications."

She then outlines the daunting issues teams face with the current system, akin to treacherous paths and unpredictable weather, building a sense of urgency and concern. As the team wonders how they'll conquer this 'mountain,' she unveils the new software, positioned as the experienced guide and state-of-the-art gear that will lead them to the summit smoothly.

This unexpected yet perfectly fitting solution turns the initial apprehension into excitement, leaving the team energized and ready to embark on this new journey, confident in their guide.

The Role of Storytelling in Different Forms of Communication

As I mentioned, storytelling is useful in all forms of communication, turning ordinary exchanges into memorable moments that stick with us long after the words are spoken or read.

In Presentations and Public Speaking

In presentations and public speaking, storytelling turns your message into a story that makes people feel something real. You can toss in a funny story from your past, share a moment that blew your mind, or even cook up a "what if" scenario that gets everyone thinking. With these stories you can turn on the little bulbs over people's heads, making your point hit home in a way they'll remember.

Take Steve Jobs's speech to Stanford grads in 2005. He didn't just stand there reeling off achievements or dishing out advice. Nope, he told stories—his own stories—about the ups and downs of his life. And just like that, everyone listening was right there with him on his journey, learning from his failures and triumphs. That speech wasn't just a talk. It was an experience, and it's stuck with people all over the globe ever since.

In the Written Word

Storytelling is like magic dust for words. It takes plain old information and turns it into something that grabs you by the heart and doesn't let go. A good tale pulls you into another realm, making you laugh, cry, or sit in awe. When you dive into a story, you're not just flipping through pages. You're stepping into someone else's shoes, living adventures you've never dreamed of, and meeting folks who feel like they could be your best buds or your worst nightmares.

J.K. Rowling is a wizard with words. She took the Harry Potter books —a series initially aimed at kids—and turned them into a worldwide obsession for readers of all ages. She wove a world so vivid and characters so real that you felt like you were hopping on the Hogwarts Express right alongside them. Rowling crafted a universe where every reader found a home, showcasing the spellbinding power of stories. With the right story, reading becomes not just a hobby, but a journey that can change the way we see the world.

In Everyday Interactions

Think about storytelling as the secret sauce that jazzes up our daily chats, turning "just another day" into "you won't believe what happened." It's like when you sit down with friends and share those "this one time" tales. Suddenly, everyone's leaning in, hooked, because your story's doing more than just recounting events—it's making everyone feel something real. When we swap stories, whether it's about that epic fail on your coffee run or something that tugged at your heartstrings, we're not just talking. We're connecting on a level that goes way beyond words.

Take "Humans of New York" as a prime example. The project started as a guy taking pictures but turned into a worldwide phenomenon just by letting everyday folks share bits of their lives. These stories, from the heartwarming to the heartbreaking, remind us that, deep down, we've all got more in common than we think. It held up a mirror to the world so that we could see not just faces, but also stories, emotions, and dreams. And that's the magic of storytelling in our everyday yakety-yak. It builds bridges where you'd least expect them, proving that a good story can make anyone, even a stranger, feel like a long-lost friend.

Storytelling in Practice: From Boardrooms to Coffee Breaks

Storytelling is not a grand, once-in-a-blue-moon kind of deal. The practice can jazz up even the most mundane Monday meeting or casual coffee break chat. Sure, it's useful for dazzling a room full of people with a mic in hand. But the true skill shines when you incorporate it into your everyday life.

Let's say you're kicking off a meeting. Instead of diving straight into the nitty-gritty, you start with a quick story about your epic fail trying to bake sourdough bread over the weekend. Suddenly, the room's lighter, people are laughing, and you've just become the most relatable person in the room. Or maybe you're trying to get to know a new colleague better. Sharing a story about the time you turned a work disaster into a win can not only showcase your problem-solving skills but also build a bridge of trust and common ground.

Everyday storytelling has its place in the digital world, too. Take LinkedIn, for example. Anyone can list their job duties in bullet points, but it takes a storytelling champ to spin those duties into a compelling narrative about leading a project, facing down challenges, and emerging victorious (or wiser). This doesn't only breathe life into your profile. It gives potential employers or connections a peek into who you are beyond the resume – your creativity, resilience, and ability to turn lemons into lemonade.

So, whether you're in the boardroom, by the watercooler, or lighting up your online presence, storytelling makes information memorable, conversations richer, and connections deeper. A good story is the bridge between just talking and truly connecting.

Overcoming Storytelling Hurdles: Mastering the Art

If you're worried that sharing a story at work might be as welcome as a skunk at a lawn party, you're not alone. Many worry that it'll come off as unprofessional or just plain unnecessary. You can dash away that fear because of the simple fact that we humans are hardwired for stories. They make everything from a client pitch to weekly team check-ins stickier—in a good way. It always brings comfort to plan for any possible challenges ahead of time so here are some common storytelling hurdles and how to vault over them without breaking a sweat:

- **The "Too Formal for Tales" Hurdle:** If you feel like your workplace is too stiff for stories the trick is to start with relevance. Connect your story directly to your point, like using a quick tale about a past project success to highlight a strategy you're proposing. You're adding color, not fluff.
- **The "Eyes Glazing Over" Hurdle:** Long-winded stories can lose your audience faster than a dropped internet connection. The solution is to keep it short and sweet. Think of your story as a tweet, not a novel. Get to the punchline or lesson before your listeners start checking their watches.
- **The "Is This Even True?" Hurdle:** If your story sounds more like a fisherman's tale, you might lose credibility. Stick to the truth, but don't be afraid to highlight the dramatic or humorous elements that naturally occurred.
- **The "Crickets" Hurdle:** Fear of no reaction, or the wrong reaction, can be paralyzing. Practice your story with a trusted friend or mentor first, getting feedback on pacing, clarity, and engagement. Knowing your story lands well in a safe space will boost your confidence for the real deal.
- **The "Lost in Translation" Hurdle:** Sometimes, the point of your story might get lost in all the theatrics. Make sure to wrap up with a clear takeaway that ties back to your initial purpose. A simple, "So, the reason I shared this is to highlight..." can ensure your message hits home.

- **The "Not the Right Time" Hurdle:** Timing is everything. Dropping a story into a high-tension meeting or a crunch-time project update might not be the best move. Gauge the room's mood and save your story for a moment when it can truly shine.

By tackling these hurdles with a mix of relevance, brevity, authenticity, practice, clarity, and timing, storytelling becomes less of a high-wire act and more of a walk in the park. And who knows? You might just find your colleagues looking forward to your next "Once upon a time at work…" This might be the case with your digital communication too. Carrying forward the art of authentic storytelling into your online interactions can make this new normal more enriching. Let's talk about it next.

10

NAVIGATE DIGITAL COMMUNICATION: THE NEW NORMAL

This digital age has shown that a tweet can spark a movement and a Zoom call can replace a boardroom. Gone are the days when communication meant face-to-face chats or long letters. Our world is turbocharged by digital chatter, making it possible to connect across continents in a blink but also turning communication into a whole new beast.

92% of adults in the U.S. are cruising the internet highways (Pew Research Center, 2021). That's a lot of scrolling, clicking, and typing! Workplaces have morphed with tools like Slack, Zoom, and Microsoft Teams, where you're more likely to "meet" your colleague in a virtual chat room than at the coffee machine. In the social sphere, a well-placed emoji or meme in your DMs can say more than a thousand words.

But with great power comes great responsibility—and a bit of a learning curve. Adapting to digital communication means understanding its pace (fast), its tone (varies from LOLs to formal proposals), and its tools (ever-evolving). To not just survive but thrive in the digital dialogue jungle, you must:

1. **Embrace Brevity and Clarity:** Digital folks are often multitaskers, so get to the point quickly. Whether it's an email, a Slack message, or a tweet, clear and concise wins the race.
2. **Read the (Virtual) Room:** Tone can be tricky online. What reads as funny in your head can land differently on screen. Use emojis and gifs wisely to add flavor or clarify sentiment, but keep your audience in mind—what works for Instagram may not fly in a professional email. Additionally, the use of emojis and gifs is a language that varies from one digital 'neighborhood' to another. A thumbs-up emoji might be a casual "okay" to some but seen as dismissive to others. When in doubt, keep it simple.
3. **Stay Updated:** Digital platforms evolve faster than a New York minute. Keeping up with the latest features enhances your online interactions. Did you know you can poll your team on Teams or use Slack channels to organize project discussions?
4. **Engage, Don't Broadcast:** Digital communication is a two-way street. Encourage feedback, ask questions, and promote interaction. When possible, try not to just broadcast your message but also engage in a dialogue.
5. **Leverage Multimedia:** Why say it when you can show it? Use visuals, videos, and presentations to add depth to your message, especially when platforms like Instagram and Twitter are designed to make visuals shine.
6. **Practice Digital Etiquette:** Yes, it's a thing. Be respectful, avoid typing in all caps (remember, it's considered yelling), and remember, behind every avatar is a human being. Beyond the basics, good digital manners include replying promptly and steering clear of touchy subjects on public forums. Think of it as being a good digital citizen—keeping the online space comfortable for everyone.

The digital world, at its core, is about communication, right down to each pixel. Adapting traditional communication skills for the digital era and keeping a finger on the pulse of technological advances ensures that your messages not only reach their destination but have their intended impact.

The Challenges of Digital Communication

Using digital communication can be a bit like trying to have a heart-to-heart in a busy city café. A lot is going on, and so much can get lost in the shuffle. Without the usual nods, smiles, or emphatic gestures, our words can end up misunderstood and seem out of place. Remember that more than 90% of communication effectiveness comes from non-verbal cues (Statistic, 2022), which don't translate in text. As a result, something as simple as "Okay" in a text can send you spiraling, wondering if you're in trouble. That's the digital dilemma.

Speed can also have us scratching our heads in digital communication. With digital conversations flying so fast, there's ample room for misreads. That quickfire email you sent, meant to be neutral, might come across as colder or more negative than intended. It's like the digital equivalent of accidentally stepping on someone's toes—without being able to see their reaction.

There's an elephant in the room...well, inbox we must address and that's information overload. With our devices pinging every other minute with emails, notifications, and updates, it's no wonder there's a link between frequent email checks and sky-high stress levels. It's like trying to drink from a firehose—you're bound to get overwhelmed.

So, what's a digital communicator to do? First, take a breath. Then read the next section!

Strategies for Effective Digital Communication

To make sure your message doesn't get lost in the digital noise, here are smart strategies to keep your digital conversations clear, engaging, and respectful:

- **Timing is Everything:** Just because you can send that email at 2 a.m. doesn't mean you should. Pay attention to the clock, and try to send messages during reasonable hours. If you're dealing with different time zones, scheduling tools and asynchronous communication tools like Slack allow for flexible communication that respects individual work rhythms and time zones.
- **Get Visual:** A picture's worth a thousand words, and in the digital space, it's also a time-saver. Whether it's a chart, a quick snap, or a screenshot, visuals can often convey your point more effectively than text alone. Plus, they break up the monotony of a text-heavy message, adding a splash of color to your communication.
- **Personalize When Possible:** In a world of mass emails and generic updates, a little personalization goes a long way. Addressing someone by name or tailoring a message to include a personal touch can make your communication stand out and feel more genuine.
- **Subject Line Signals:** In emails, use concise, clear subject lines that immediately inform the recipient about the email's purpose. Advanced tip: include tags like [URGENT], [FYI], [REQUEST], or [RESPONSE NEEDED] at the beginning to set expectations.
- **The "BCC" Courtesy:** When sending emails to a group where recipients don't need to know each other's email addresses, use BCC (Blind Carbon Copy). It respects privacy and prevents any reply-all mishaps.
- **Acknowledge Before You Dive Deep:** When receiving an email requiring a detailed response, send a quick acknowledgment reply. A simple "Received, I'll get back to you by [specific time or day]" keeps the sender in the loop and eases anxieties about whether their message was seen.
- **Use Previews:** Ever sent an email only to spot a typo as soon as it's too late? Most email platforms offer a "preview" or "test send" feature. Use it to send the email to yourself first, giving

you a chance to catch those sneaky errors and see how your message looks in someone else's inbox.
- **Email Signature Savvy:** Keep your email signature updated and informative, including your role, company, and best contact method. However, avoid overloading it with unnecessary details, quotes, or images that can clutter the message.
- **Virtual Meeting Mute Etiquette:** In video calls, make it a habit to mute yourself when not speaking. Background noise, from keyboard typing to other conversations, can be distracting and disrupt the flow of the meeting. Additionally, ensure that your audio quality is set up to enhance your input when you unmute yourself to speak.
- **Camera On, Engagement Up:** Turning your camera on during video meetings shows engagement and presence, creating a more connected and interactive session. Treat it like a face-to-face meeting and make "eye contact" by looking at the camera, not your screen. Use nods and smiles to show you're engaged, even if you're on mute. And a pro tip: make sure your lighting makes you look more like a professional and less like a mysterious figure lurking in the shadows. However, it's also respectful to inform participants in advance if camera usage is expected.
- **Respect the Chat:** In virtual meetings, using the chat feature can be a great way to contribute without interrupting. But remember, keep comments professional and relevant to the discussion, as side conversations can distract from the main topic.
- **Digital Handshake:** In online networking, a personalized connection request or introduction is like a handshake. Avoid generic messages; a brief note on why you're reaching out can set the tone for a meaningful professional relationship.
- **Closing Conversations Gracefully:** Whether in email threads or instant messaging, provide clear closure to conversations. A simple "Thank you for the information. I

have everything I need to proceed," can prevent unnecessary follow-ups and shows respect for the other person's time.

Tools and Platforms for Enhancing Digital Communication

Having the right tools and platforms for communication at your fingertips makes life a whole lot easier:

- **Email's New Best Friends:** Ever felt like your inbox is a black hole? Tools like Boomerang or Mailtrack turn an email into a boomerang that comes back, letting you know when your message is read and even reminding you to follow up.
- **The Meeting Magicians:** Zoom, Microsoft Teams, and Google Meet have become the new meeting rooms, coffee shops, and sometimes, the after-work hangout spot. They're the go-betweens that keep us connected, making video calls smoother than your morning latte. With features like screen sharing, virtual backgrounds, and breakout rooms, they've turned online meetings from a headache into a highlight.
- **The Collaboration Wizards:** Say goodbye to endless back-and-forth emails. Platforms like Slack and Asana make teamwork feel like less work. They're the digital equivalent of a brainstorming session, where ideas flow freely, tasks are clear, and updates are instant. Whether you're planning a project or just catching up, these tools keep everyone on the same page.
- **The Social Butterflies:** Social media platforms like LinkedIn, Twitter, and Instagram aren't just for selfies and snacks. They're networking goldmines, places to share your thoughts, showcase your work, and connect with others in your field. Think of them as a professional conference you can attend in your pajamas.
- **The Personal Touch:** In a world of texts and tweets, personalization platforms like Canva and Loom add a personal touch. Canva helps your messages stand out with custom designs, while Loom lets you send video messages

when an email won't cut it. They allow you to make your communications as unique as you are.

The Future of Digital Communication

Peeking into the future of digital communication is like glimpsing into a sci-fi novel come to life. With every leap in technology, the ways we connect and converse online are getting a major upgrade. Slipping on a VR headset allows you to sit in your living room yet still be transported to your next team meeting. Suddenly, you're all in the same virtual room, brainstorming on a digital whiteboard. That's the promise of platforms like Spatial, turning dull video calls into immersive experiences where ideas can literally float in the air around you.

Then, there's AI, an ever-ready assistant, stepping up its game beyond simple tasks to becoming a cornerstone of customer interaction. Chatbots like Drift and Intercom are already holding down the fort, answering questions and solving problems at all hours, making sure no customer feels left in the digital void. This goes beyond convenience to weave a tighter, more responsive form of connection between businesses and their audiences.

As we march into this brave new world, our playbook for digital communication needs to evolve. Staying curious, embracing the new tools and platforms as they come, and always being ready to learn will be your guiding stars. Being adaptable isn't just an advantage. It's become a necessity. Turning the page from the futuristic vistas of digital communication, we're reminded that at the end of the day, technology is just a tool, and the true magic lies in our human touch.

11

THE ART OF CONVERSING: LEARNING TO TALK TO ANYONE, ANYWHERE

Good chit-chat doesn't just fill awkward silences or allow for making small talk at parties. Being a good conversationalist as part of your social toolkit opens doors, forges new relationships, and even gives your social standing a boost. Whether you're networking in a professional setting, bonding over coffee, or even striking up a convo in an online forum, the ability to start and keep a conversation going is golden.

Why? Because conversations are the bridges we build between ourselves and the world. They're how we share ideas, learn from others, and connect on a level deeper than just "liking" a post or sending an emoji. For instance, imagine you're at a networking event, feeling like a wallflower with your drink in hand. The moment you muster up the courage to join a conversation, ask questions, and share a bit about yourself, you're not just another face in the crowd. You're a storyteller, a listener, and someone people want to know more about.

If breaking out of the wallflower mold is something you struggle with, I have great news for you. The art of conversation is something anyone can learn. While some people are born with a silver tongue, even they need to practice so that they don't lose the talent. Along with practicing conversation regularly, being a good conversationalist means that you need to be genuinely interested in others and be ready to put yourself out there even when you don't feel like you're ready.

Conversations are part of what makes us human. They're how friendships are born, ideas are sparked, and sometimes, they're how revolutions start. Through the simple act of talking and listening, we break down barriers, find common ground, and build a world that's a little more connected. So next time you have the chance to start a conversation, take it. Who knows where it might lead?

Breaking the Ice: Starting Conversations

Ever wondered where the term "breaking the ice" came from? Back in the day, when ships were stuck in frozen waters, smaller vessels called icebreakers would come along to clear a path. Once that path was clear, though, other ships could follow with ease. That's a lot like conversations, especially the daunting task of starting one. Being the first to speak up, to "break the ice," sets the stage for others to join in, making everything that follows a bit smoother.

Let's be real, initiating a chat, especially with someone you don't know well, can feel like stepping onto a stage with a spotlight glaring down at you. I take comfort in assuming that the person on the other end might be waiting for someone to break that ice too. Sometimes, I've got to be the icebreaker, steering the ship through the frosty silence. That role might fall on you too.

This begs the question of how to dive in without belly-flopping. Shared experiences are your lifeline here. At a networking bash, dropping a line about the keynote speech or even the wild choice of venue décor can open doors. It's about finding that common ground, however small, to start building a bridge.

Or, why not go with an open-ended question? These are your "tell me more" invitations beckon the other person to share their thoughts and stories. Swap out the "Did you like the speaker?" with a "What did you think about the speaker's views on innovation?" Boom, you've just opened a door to a real conversation, not just polite nods.

Don't underestimate the power of a genuine compliment either. Spotting something to compliment, be it someone's keen insights during a session or their standout presentation skills, can warm up the conversation faster than a sunny day melts ice. Just make sure it's sincere. Authenticity makes the other person feel valued and more prone to opening up.

The next time you find yourself on the edge of a conversation, remember that breaking the ice isn't just about getting through the initial chill. You're laying the foundation for a connection that could lead to who knows where. Be bold, be curious, and most importantly, be yourself. The best conversations start when we let our guards down and simply connect.

Maintaining the Momentum: Sustaining Conversations

So, you've broken the ice, shared a laugh, or nodded in agreement about the keynote speaker's wild anecdotes. What now? How do you keep the chat from fizzling out faster than a soda left in the sun? Here are some tips and tricks to keep the conversation flowing:

Be a Pro Listener

Actively listen to what the other person is saying. Many of us make the mistake of waiting for our turn to talk without really tuning in to what the other person is saying. Nod along, throw in a "Really?" or "Then what happened?" to show you're with them every step of the way. For instance, if they're talking about a recent trip, ask about the best meal they had or the craziest thing they saw. It shows you're listening and interested in the details.

Ask Follow-Up Questions

Questions are the fuel that keeps conversations burning. If someone mentions they love hiking, don't just stop at "That's cool." Dive deeper with, "What's the best trail you've ever conquered?" or "Got any hiking spots to recommend?" It keeps the door open for more shared stories and insights.

Share, Don't Overshare

Balance is key. While it's great to share bits about yourself, keep the spotlight rotating. If you've just told a story about your most epic kitchen fail, flip the script and ask about their cooking adventures (or misadventures). It's like a tennis match—back and forth.

Find Common Ground

Discovering shared interests or experiences makes you and your conversation partner feel related. Maybe you both geek out over vintage comic books or share a secret passion for bad reality TV. These commonalities are stepping stones to deeper, more engaging dialogues.

Embrace the Awkward Pauses

Every conversation has its ups and downs. Instead of panicking when there's a lull, use it as a chance to steer the chat in a new direction. A simple "Speaking of which, have you heard about..." can refresh the conversation and bring in new energy. The next section shares more insight on using silences in conversation to your advantage.

Know When to Wrap It Up

Just like a good movie, every conversation has its end. Recognizing when to gracefully exit is just as important as keeping it going. A simple "I've enjoyed talking about our jungle survival tactics, but I've got to catch another session now" leaves things on a positive note and opens the door for future chats.

Navigating Through Awkward Silences

Awkward silences in conversations are like hitting a pothole on the road of chatter – jarring, unexpected, and sometimes making you wish you could just teleport to another place. Still, with a bit of savvy, you can keep going. Silences happen for all sorts of reasons—maybe someone's digesting what's just been said, or perhaps you've both hit a topic that's a dead-end. The trick is not to panic but to see it as an opportunity to steer the conversation in a new, more interesting direction. Here are five strategies to help you do just that, without shifting gears and changing the topic:

1. **Crack a Light Joke:** Humor is like a universal solvent—it can dissolve tension and fill those silent gaps. However, it's got to fit the moment. If you're discussing work, a light, work-related joke can ease the lull. Just dropped a fact that met with crickets? Crack a smile and say, "Well, I found that fascinating... I'll be here all week, folks!" Keep it light and make sure it's something that won't step on toes.
2. **Embrace the Pause:** Sometimes, silence isn't awkward. It's just a breathing space. Acknowledge it with a relaxed comment like, "It's nice to have a moment to think, isn't it?" This can take the pressure off and make the silence feel more comfortable, showing you're cool with the ebb and flow of conversation.
3. **Reflect on What Was Said:** Use the pause as a chance to reflect on the last topic. "You know, thinking more about what you said earlier..." This shows you're engaged and compliments the other person. You're essentially letting them know that their thoughts are worth pondering.
4. **Ask for Their Opinion:** People love to share their thoughts. If you've hit a pause, pivot by asking for their take on something relevant. "I've been pondering X lately—what's your take on it?" This move shows you value their insight and turns the silence into a launchpad for deeper discussion.
5. **Share a Quick Anecdote:** If the conversation's stalled, a brief, related story from your own experience can reignite interest. "That reminds me of the time I..." Just make sure it's short and ties back to the conversation, so it feels like a natural flow rather than a random detour.

Awkward silences don't have to be the end of the road for a conversation. In fact, navigating through them is a skill, one that gets easier with practice. With a bit of creativity, empathy, and willingness to lean into the quiet, you can find even more meaningful dialogue on the other side of the quiet. Every conversation is a journey, and sometimes, it's the unexpected detours that lead to the most memorable destinations.

Mastering Small Talk: The Building Block of Conversations

Small talk is the appetizer to the main conversation course. You wouldn't serve a heavy stew without a light salad first, right? Topics like "Did you catch the game last night?" or "How was your weekend?" are your salad. They're easy to digest, generally enjoyable, and a safe bet for most people. To make effective small talk, you've got to tune into the other person's energy. If they're wearing a sports jersey, maybe sports is a go-to topic. If they mention they're into movies, ask about films they've enjoyed recently.

Small talk is your entry ticket to deeper, more substantial conversations. It's where first impressions are made and where professional relationships begin to take root. So, it's worth the investment in learning to do it effectively. Consider these tips to elevate your small talk game and turn even the most casual chats into engaging exchanges:

- **Stay Current:** Keep a mental list of light, engaging topics. Read up on a variety of subjects so you can easily connect with different people.
- **Use Their Name:** It's a small touch but using someone's name in conversation makes it more personal and engaging.
- **Embrace the Power of Observation:** Before you even say hello, take a moment to observe. Maybe the person has an interesting piece of jewelry, a book in hand, or a unique phone case. Starting with a genuine compliment or question about something you've noticed can kick off the conversation

on a positive and curious note. For instance, "That's a fascinating watch! Does it have a story behind it?"
- **Leverage Your Environment:** Whether you're at a conference, a coffee shop, or a community event, your surroundings are ripe with conversation starters. Comment on the artwork on the walls, the architecture, or even the playlist that's setting the mood. "I love how this place has a retro feel to it. Do you come here often?"
- **Share a Fun Fact:** Have a collection of interesting, light-hearted facts in your back pocket ready to spark curiosity and smiles. "Did you know that honey never spoils? Archaeologists have found pots of honey in ancient Egyptian tombs that are over 3,000 years old and still good!"
- **The 'Future Plan' Inquiry:** Instead of the typical "What do you do?" question, try asking about plans or dreams. "Is there a skill you've always wanted to learn or a place you've dreamed of visiting?" This can lead to discovering mutual interests or ambitions.
- **Play the 'Favorites' Game:** Asking about favorites is a simple yet effective way to dive into someone's interests and preferences without getting too personal. "What's your favorite movie genre, and why?" or "Do you have a favorite local restaurant?" Everyone loves to share their favorites, and it's a great way to find common ground.
- **Utilize the 'Two Things' Technique:** When sharing about yourself, offer two things instead of one. "This weekend, I'm planning to go hiking and try out a new sushi spot." It gives the other person two potential topics to latch onto and ask more about.

Conversing Across Cultures: Embracing Diversity

Chatting across cultures is like being a world traveler from the comfort of your conversation. In today's global village, being able to nimbly navigate a chat with someone from a different background is a must-have skill.

Doing so means that you must first recognize that not everyone talks shop the way you do. For instance, while you might appreciate straight talk, as often admired in places like Germany or the Netherlands, on the other side of the globe in Japan or South Korea, folks might take a more roundabout path to get their point across. In that situation, you're not tiptoeing around the point. You're showing respect for the harmony of the conversation.

And speaking of respect, it's the golden rule of cross-cultural talks. Dive into the do's and don'ts of cultural norms like a detective. A firm handshake here, a bow there, or even understanding when and where to pull out your business card can make all the difference. It's about showing that you value not just the chat but the person you're chatting with.

Here's a tip: try learning a word or two in the other person's language. It shows appreciation for where the other person is coming from. With apps like Duolingo or Babbel, picking up a few greetings or thank-yous is easier than ever.

Learning to converse across cultures isn't strictly about avoiding faux pas – although that benefit is great! The skill opens up new perspectives and, let's be honest, makes for some pretty fantastic stories.

Overcoming Communication Barriers: Talking to Difficult People

Conversations do not always go as we expect. Sometimes, we have to chat with someone who is the kind of person who might not be the easiest to crack a smile, who might seem a bit set in their ways, or who just doesn't warm up easily. I'm not setting them up to be villains here, just folks who, for whatever reason, present a bit more of a challenge in the communication department.

Talking to someone like this might make you instinctively want to put your guard up but try to approach these chats with a hefty dose of patience and a truckload of empathy. Instead of mirroring their frostiness or getting defensive, try to see the world from behind their eyes for a moment. Maybe they're having a rough day, or perhaps life's dealt them a few too many blows lately. A little kindness can go a long way, even if it's not immediately returned.

When it comes to sharing your side of things, be assertive. Get your point across firmly but in a respectful way. "I understand where you're coming from, but here's how I see it..." is a good place to start.

Let's be real. Sometimes, despite your best efforts, the conversation just isn't going anywhere good. If you've tried to bridge the gap and they're still building walls, it might be time to gracefully bow out. "It seems we're not going to see eye-to-eye on this. Maybe we can revisit it another time," is a polite way to hit the pause button. While you can't control how someone else behaves, you're the boss of your reactions.

Dealing with challenging communicators isn't about winning or losing. The aim is to handle the situation with as much grace and understanding as you can muster, knowing when to push a little and when to ease off the gas. With a bit of time and patience, maybe, just maybe, today's tough nut to crack could be tomorrow's great conversation partner.

Adapting Communication Styles: Different Strokes for Different Folks

We don't all converse in the same way. Recognizing and adapting to the varied ways people express themselves is necessary to make these exchanges as smooth, effective, and productive as possible.

Maybe you're the kind of person who loves to dive deep into details, sharing every layer of the story. What happens if you're talking to someone who prefers their information concise and to the point? In situations like this, it's helpful to streamline your storytelling, providing just the key points to keep them engaged and the conversation moving forward.

Adapting your communication style doesn't mean you're being inauthentic. Rather, it's about being considerate of how the other person processes information. Flexibility in how you communicate makes you more approachable and relatable to a wider circle of people.

To harness the skill of communication adaptation:

- **Observe and Adjust**: Pay attention to the other person's style. Are their messages brief? Do they get straight to the point, or do they enjoy a more narrative approach? Adjust your style to better align with theirs.
- **Be Direct or Expand as Needed**: If they appreciate brevity, keep your responses short and focused. If they're more detail-oriented, feel free to elaborate more than you might usually.
- **Clarify Preferences**: Especially in work contexts, it's okay to ask how someone prefers to communicate. Do they like email updates, or would they prefer a quick call? Knowing this saves time and misunderstandings.

Many people think good conversation is a thing of the past, blaming it on our obsession with screens and short texts. The truth is, too many of us are just not doing it right. I hope this chapter impacted you on how you can bring real, heart-to-heart chats back to life with a few simple tweaks. With that topic wrapped up, we have now reached the end of this discussion on effective communication in the workplace.

I hope you've been enjoying this incredible resource. Here's the thing - your experience can be even more fulfilling, and it all starts with a simple question: How can you help others on their journey to become more effective with their communication?

Leaving a review for this book isn't just about sharing your thoughts; it's an opportunity to deliver value to others who are seeking guidance and inspiration. Your words can make a difference in someone else's experience.

1. Click the link or scan the QR code below to leave an honest review on Amazon.

2. Share your thoughts, insights, and how this book has impacted your journey.

By leaving a review, you're not just helping me; you're paying it forward to others who are on their path to becoming more effective communicators. Your words of wisdom can inspire and guide them, making their journey smoother and more fulfilling.

So, let's come together as a community, share our experiences, and help each other thrive.

CONCLUSION

As we turn the final page of this journey together, it's time to look back at the terrain we've covered and the treasures we've gathered along the way. Effective communication isn't just about talking louder or more. Often, it's not even about what we say. When accounting for both what's said and expressed nonverbally, effective communication allows us to create deeper connections, understand each other better, and express ourselves more truly.

While some people are naturally better at communicating than others, it's something anyone can learn with time and dedication. You've made it to these final pages, showing that you are indeed keen on mastering the art and science that is effective communication. As you continue to practice, know that this skill will dramatically transform your personal and professional relationships and pave the way for success in every aspect of your life.

From the foundational stones of communication to the advanced techniques that give our words wings, we've covered a lot. We started by laying the groundwork with the basic principles of communication, understanding the pivotal role of social intelligence, and navigating through common barriers that often silence our best intentions. We ventured into the diverse realms of non-verbal, verbal, and written communication, uncovering the strategies that make each mode effective.

We then scaled the heights of advanced communication skills, where the power of self-confidence and the magic of storytelling reign supreme, enriching our conversations and presentations with depth and dynamism. And we didn't stop there. We explored special topics like digital communication and cultural sensitivity, which are essential in our global, interconnected world.

The main takeaways from our journey are clear:

- The heart of effective communication beats with active listening and empathy.
- Non-verbal cues are the silent but expressive partners of our words.
- Clarity and tone in verbal and written communication are non-negotiable for true understanding.
- Confidence is the backbone of impactful communication.
- Storytelling is our most engaging and memorable ally.
- The digital age requires a fresh playbook for communication.
- The art of conversation is universal, allowing us to initiate and maintain connections across any divide.

If you ever need a refresher on any of these topics covered, don't be afraid to revisit these pages. After all, this guide was designed to be a quick reference no matter where you are on your path to becoming a better communicator. Be confident in the fact that you're equipped with practical exercises and strategies, designed not as one-time tasks but as stepping stones to a richer, more connected way of living. Mastering effective communication is a lifelong journey, filled with moments of triumph and challenge, each requiring patience, practice, and a dash of courage. So don't let occasional hiccups along the way derail your progress. Keep on learning. Even mistakes are lessons.

The path lies open for you to take these lessons into the world. Start small, perhaps by practicing active listening in your next chat or weaving a story into your upcoming presentation. Each step, no matter how small, is a step toward a more allied, confident you.

As we part ways, remember that effective communication is more than a skill—it's a way of being. With the tools and insights from this book, you're well on your way to not just speaking but truly connecting. May this guide be your companion as you navigate the rich landscapes of human interaction as you become more comfortable with building bridges, forging bonds, and sharing the unique light of your voice with the world.

Here's to your journey in mastering the art of communication. May every word you speak and listen to bring you closer to the heart of what it means to truly connect.

ABOUT THE AUTHOR

Born in a quaint New England town, Marguerite has carved a remarkable path in the professional realm, boasting over two decades of unparalleled leadership. Now 44 and residing in New Jersey with her supportive husband and two beautiful children, her journey has seen her evolve from the humble beginnings of her hometown, through the corporate corridors of Chicago, and into the dynamic streets of New York. Throughout this journey, Marguerite has held several esteemed leadership roles in both large and small organizations, consistently breaking through glass ceilings and challenging the status quo.

Witnessing firsthand the untapped potential of countless talented women who were often overlooked in the corporate world, Marguerite's keen observations and personal experiences ignited a deep passion within her. This led to the creation of her debut work, "Fearless Female Leadership," a meticulously researched and engagingly written book that celebrates the unique prowess of women in leadership. In this book, she masterfully intertwines thought-provoking insights with compelling narratives, spotlighting the unique strengths and struggles of women in positions of power.

With her latest book, "Impactful Inclusive Leadership," Marguerite broadens her scope beyond championing women's potential. She dives into the essential tenets of Diversity, Equity, and Inclusion (DEI), crafting a compelling call to action. This work urges leaders of all stripes to cultivate truly inclusive environments where diversity is celebrated, and equity is a foundational principle.

Marguerite Allolding stands not only as an advocate for change but as a beacon of hope and an embodiment of the transformative power of leadership that is both fearless and inclusive. Her unwavering commitment to empowering women and advocating for DEI inspires everyone to strive for a world that thrives on the pillars of equity and inclusion and recognizes the strength in diversity.

Founder and CEO of SHE LEADS STRATEGIES
https://www.SHELEADSSTRATEGIES.com

ALSO BY MARGUERITE ALLOLDING

Also by Marguerite Allolding

9 ESSENTIAL STRATEGIES TO OVERCOME **GENDER BIASES,** BUILD **CONFIDENCE AND** EMPOWER **YOUR CAREER**

FEARLESS FEMALE LEADERSHIP

MARGUERITE ALLOLDING

Click link or scan QR code below to find Fearless Female Leadership: 9 Essential Strategies to overcome Gender Biases, Build Confidence and Empower Your career.

Also by Marguerite Allolding

IMPACTFUL INCLUSIVE LEADERSHIP
MARGUERITE ALLOLDING

Click link or scan QR code below to find IMPACTFUL INCLUSIVE LEADERSHIP: 9 Powerful Strategies That Encourage Diversity, Foster Equity, and Cultivate Inclusivity to Transform Your Workplace.

Also by Marguerite Allolding

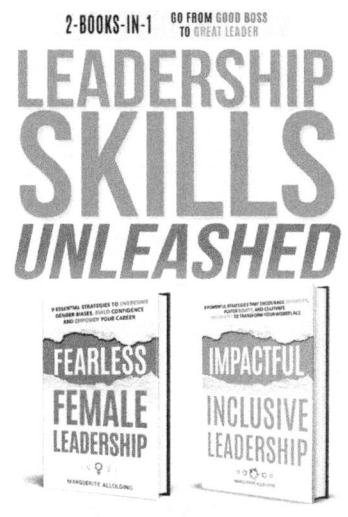

Click link or scan QR code below to find Leadership Skills Unleashed: 18 Transformative Strategies for Managers at Any Level – Develop a Growth Mindset, Overcome Imposter Syndrome, and Create a Culture of Belonging

REFERENCES

A 10-second pause that changed history | ASU News. https://news.asu.edu/20230111-discoveries-10second-pause-changed-history

Admin, & Admin. (2023, September 19). *Self-Efficacy Theory. Communication Theory.* https://www.communicationtheory.org/self-efficacy-theory/

Abpp, S. K. W. P. (2020, December 11). *Put active listening together with empathy to improve your relationships.* Psychology Today. https://www.psychologytoday.com/us/blog/fulfillment-any-age/201203/11-ways-active-listening-can-help-your-relationships

American Marketing Association. (2024, January 22). *The Art of the Narrative Arc: Why Marketers Must Learn to be Storytellers.* https://www.ama.org/marketing-news/the-art-of-the-narrative-arc-why-marketers-must-learn-to-be-storytellers/

Are there universal facial expressions? - Paul Ekman Group. (2021, November 22). Paul Ekman Group. https://www.paulekman.com/resources/universal-facial-expressions/

Author, N. (2020, May 30). *Search and email still top the list of most popular online activities | Pew Research Center.* Pew Research Center: Internet, Science & Tech. https://www.pewresearch.org/internet/2011/08/09/search-and-email-still-top-the-list-of-most-popular-online-activities/

Baker, C. (2023, July 28). *14 Amazon Leadership Principles and Why They Matter.* Leaders.com. https://leaders.com/articles/leadership/amazon-leadership-principles/

Belludi, N. (2017, October 27). *Albert Mehrabian's 7-38-55 Rule of Personal Communication - Right Attitudes.* Right Attitudes. https://www.rightattitudes.com/2008/10/04/7-38-55-rule-personal-communication/

Camarote, R. (2021, January 5). *Elon Musk is a master at communication. Here are his 3 secrets to getting the message across.* Inc.com. https://www.inc.com/robin-camarote/if-you-want-to-improve-communication-take-a-look-a.html

Chaffey, D. (2022, November 4). *Golden circle model: Sinek's theory value proposition: start with why.* https://www.smartinsights.com/digital-marketing-strategy/online-value-proposition/start-with-why-creating-a-value-proposition-with-the-golden-circle-model/

Coronado-Maldonado, I., & Benítez-Márquez, M. D. (2023). *Emotional intelligence, leadership, and work teams: A hybrid literature review.* Heliyon, 9(10), e20356. https://doi.org/10.1016/j.heliyon.2023.e20356

CPP Inc. (n.d.). © Copyright 2009 CPP, Inc. https://shop.themyersbriggs.com/PRESS/Workplace_Conflict_Study.aspx

Creativite Consultants, V. a. P. B. (2019, May 30). *The Pixar Pitch. Story-selling at its best. . ..* WordPress.com. https://creativite-consultants.com/2019/05/30/the-pixar-pitch-story-selling-at-its-best/

Dawley, D. D., & Anthony, W. P. (2003). *User perceptions of E-Mail at work. Journal of Business and Technical Communication, 17*(2), 170–200. https://doi.org/10.1177/1050651902250947

Detert, J. R. (2022, April 18). *Why employees are afraid to speak.* Harvard Business Review. https://hbr.org/2007/05/why-employees-are-afraid-to-speak

DarshMam. (2020, June 7). *Positive and negative effects of technology on academic writing skills.* HackerNoon. https://hackernoon.com/positive-and-negative-effects-of-technology-on-academic-writing-skills-fw3430lq

Don't start your next email with this phrase | Maryland Smith. https://www.rhsmith.umd.edu/research/dont-start-your-next-email-phrase

Dean, D. J., PhD. (2019, April 20). *Can You Hear Me Now: What role does active listening at work play and how can we improve?* https://www.linkedin.com/pulse/can-you-hear-me-now-what-role-does-active-listening-debra-j

Emcworthy. *Cultural dimensions – hall, verbal and nonverbal.* Pressbooks. https://kirkwood.pressbooks.pub/emcworthy/chapter/cultural-dimensions/

Frith, C. D. (2009). Role of facial expressions in social interactions. *Philosophical Transactions of the Royal Society B, 364*(1535), 3453–3458. https://doi.org/10.1098/rstb.2009.0142

Goleman, D. (2022, September 22). *Primal leadership: the hidden driver of great performance.* Harvard Business Review. https://hbr.org/2001/12/primal-leadership-the-hidden-driver-of-great-performance

Gothelf, J. *The power of storytelling [Video].* TED Talks. https://www.ted.com/talks/jeff_gothelf_the_power_of_storytelling?hasSummary=true

Grammarly. (2022, October 28). *Demand for writing skills soars, but support lags behind | Grammarly. Demand for Writing Skills Soars, but Support Lags Behind | Grammarly.* https://www.grammarly.com/blog/demand-for-strong-written-communication-skills-is-soaring-why-isnt-the-support/

Heilpern, W. (2016, August 12). *Richard Branson told us his most surprising character trait.* Business Insider. https://www.businessinsider.com/richard-branson-talks-about-public-speaking-2016-8

Hooker, J. N. (2012). *Cultural differences in business communication.* ResearchGate. https://www.researchgate.net/publication/260898153_Cultural_differences_in_business_communication

How stories change the brain. Greater Good. https://greatergood.berkeley.edu/article/item/how_stories_change_brain

Jettisoning work email reduces stress. (2012, May 3). UCI News. https://news.uci.edu/2012/05/03/jettisoning-work-email-reduces-stress/

Malyk, M. (2023, November 13). *10 Examples of unconscious bias in the workplace and how to avoid them.* https://www.easyllama.com/blog/unconscious-bias-in-the-workplace/

MindTools. *Develop your personal wellbeing and career skills - Mind Tools - Mind Tools.* https://www.mindtools.com/ao9kek8/mehrabians-communication-model

Ms, T. G. L. (2023, October 27). *4 ways to adapt the way you communicate to different situations.* wikiHow. https://www.wikihow.com/Adapt-the-Way-You-Communicate-to-Different-Situations

Ollerton, M. (2023, November 29). *The imperative of effective communication in the workplace.* Workplace Languages. https://www.workplacelanguages.com/effective-communication/

Prast, I. (2023, September 4). *Writing for different audiences: Adapting your tone and style.* Medium. https://medium.com/@irfanmuhammad9192/writing-for-different-audiences-adapting-your-tone-and-style-e76d896745c

Pew Research Center. (2021, April 7). *Social media usage in the U.S. in 2019 | Pew Research Center.* https://www.pewresearch.org/short-reads/2019/04/10/share-of-u-s-adults-using-social-media-including-facebook-is-mostly-unchanged-since-2018/

PREPROTIC, M. (2023, March 6). *10 tips for effective cross-cultural communication.* Plecto. https://www.plecto.com/blog/motivation/cross-cultural-communication/

Presentations, B. F. (2022, April 20). *6 ways Tony Robbins masters public speaking.* Big FishPresentations. https://bigfishpresentations.com/2016/08/12/6-ways-tony-robbins-masters-public-speaking/

Royle, O. R. (2023, October 18). *Microsoft CEO Satya Nadella does not see empathy as a soft skill: 'It's the hardest skill we learn.'* Fortune. https://fortune.com/2023/10/18/microsoft-ceo-satya-nadella-empathy-soft-skill/

Sabater, V. (2023, March 15). *Daniel Goleman's Social Intelligence Theory.* Exploring Your Mind. https://exploringyourmind.com/daniel-golemans-social-intelligence-theory/

Smart Chaffey, D. (2024, January 24). *Golden Circle model: Sinek's theory value proposition: start with why.* Smart Insights. https://www.smartinsights.com/digital-marketing-strategy/online-value-proposition/start-with-why-creating-a-value-proposition-with-the-golden-circle-model/

Smith, M., MA. (2024, February 5). *Nonverbal communication and body language.* HelpGuide.org. https://www.helpguide.org/articles/relationships-communication/nonverbal-communication.htm

Staff, C. (2023, December 1). *7 ways to improve your writing skills.* Coursera. https://www.coursera.org/articles/writing-skills

Staff, L. E. (2023, August 21). *The importance of empathy in the workplace.* CCL. https://www.ccl.org/articles/leading-effectively-articles/empathy-in-the-workplace-a-tool-for-effective-leadership/

Statista. (2023, August 22). *Number of e-mails per day worldwide 2017-2026.* https://www.statista.com/statistics/456500/daily-number-of-e-mails-worldwide/

Stevens, E. *The 6 best icebreakers for your next meeting or workshop.* https://www.workshopper.com/post/icebreakers-for-meetings-and-workshops

Street, F. (2021, February 5). *Carol Dweck: A Summary of Growth and Fixed Mindsets.* Farnam Street. https://fs.blog/carol-dweck-mindset/

Sullivan, B., & Thompson, H. (2013, May 3). *Opinion | A focus on distraction.* The New York Times. https://www.nytimes.com/2013/05/05/opinion/sunday/a-focus-on-distraction.html

References

TED. (2012, October 1). *Your body language may shape who you are | Amy Cuddy | TED [Video]*. YouTube. https://www.youtube.com/watch?v=Ks-_Mh1QhMc

The 5 Love Languages: The Secret to Love That Lasts: Gary Chapman: 9780802473158: Amazon.com: Books. https://www.amazon.com/Love-Languages-Secret-That-Lasts/dp/0802473156

The MIT Press Reader. (2020, January 13). *Proxemics 101: Understanding Personal Space across Cultures*. https://thereader.mitpress.mit.edu/understanding-personal-space-proxemics/

Van Zant, A. B., & Berger, J. (2019, June 13). *How the Voice Persuades*. Journal of Personality and Social Psychology. Advance online publication. http://dx.doi.org/10.1037/pspi0000193

Vilkė, V. (2023, August 30). *Behind the silence: Why employees choose not to speak up*. https://www.linkedin.com/pulse/behind-silence-why-employees-choose-speak-up-viktorija-vilk%C4%97

Yate, M. (2023, December 21). *The importance of written communication skills*. SHRM. https://www.shrm.org/topics-tools/news/career-advice-qa/importance-written-communication-skills

Zafar, Y. (2023, April 6). *"The Art of Storytelling: How to Make your LinkedIn Profile Stand Out."* https://www.linkedin.com/pulse/art-storytelling-how-make-your-linkedin-profile-stand-yousuf-zafar

Zak, P. J. (2015, February 1). *Why inspiring stories make us react: The neuroscience of narrative*. PubMed Central (PMC). https://www.ncbi.nlm.nih.gov/pmc/articles/PMC4445577/

Made in the USA
Middletown, DE
17 June 2024